COMMUNICATOR I

The Comprehensive Course in Functional English

Steven J. Molinsky
Bill Bliss

Contributing Authors

Susan Siegel
Carol Piñeiro

Prentice Hall Regents
Upper Saddle River, New Jersey 07458

Library of Congress Cataloguing-in-Publication Data

Molinsky, Steven J.
    Communicator 1 : the comprehensive course in functional English /
Steven J. Molinsky, Bill Bliss
       p. cm.
    Includes index.
    ISBN 0-13-301649-8
    1. English language—Textbooks for foreign speakers.   I. Bliss,
Bill.   II. Title.
PE1128.M672   1994
428.2'8—dc20
                                              94-20249
                                               CIP

Publisher: Tina Carver
Director of Production and Manufacturing: David Riccardi
Editorial Production/Design Manager: Dominick Mosco
Production Supervision: Janet Johnston
Page Composition: Ken Liao
Production Coordinator: Ray Keating
Cover Coordinator: Merle Krumper

Cover Designer: Marianne Frasco
Cover Art: Todd Ware
Interior Design: Kenny Beck

Photographs: Paul Tañedo
Illustrations: Richard E. Hill

© 1995 by Prentice Hall
Prentice-Hall, Inc.
Simon & Schuster / A Viacom Company
Upper Saddle River, New Jersey 07458

Printed in the United States of America

10   9   8   7   6   5

ISBN 0-13-301649-8

Prentice-Hall International (UK) Limited, London
Prentice-Hall of Australia Pty. Limited, Sydney
Prentice-Hall Canada Inc., Toronto
Prentice-Hall Hispanoamericana, S.A., Mexico
Prentice-Hall of India Private Limited, New Delhi
Prentice-Hall of Japan, Inc., Tokyo
Simon & Schuster Asia Pte. Ltd., Singapore
Editora Prentice-Hall do Brasil, Ltda., Rio de Janeiro

Contents

To the Teacher   v

Components of a *Communicator* Lesson   viii

1   **Meeting and Greeting People**   1

2   **Sharing News and Information**   15
     Describing People

3   **Describing Things and Places**   33
     Reporting Information
     Remembering and Forgetting

4   **Requests**   53
     Directions and Instructions
     Checking Understanding
     Asking for Repetition

5   **Complimenting**   67
     Satisfaction and Dissatisfaction
     Likes and Dislikes

6   **Preferences**   85
     Wants and Desires

7   **Promises**   105
     Intentions

8   **Offering Help**   127
     Gratitude and Appreciation

9   **Permission**   145

Notes and Commentary   169

Inventory of Functions and Conversation Strategies   175

Scripts for Listening Exercises   180

Index   184

Communicator is a functional English course for adult and secondary school learners of English. It is intended for students who have been exposed to the essentials of intermediate-level grammar and who have already mastered the usage of English for everyday life situations. The text builds upon and reinforces this foundation and prepares students for higher-level language skills required for effective interpersonal communication. *Communicator* is organized functionally and incorporates integrated coverage of grammar and topics.

The Dimensions of Communication: Function, Form, and Content

Communicator provides dynamic, communicative practice that involves students in lively interactions based on the content of real-life contexts and situations. Every lesson offers students simultaneous practice with one or more functions, the grammatical forms needed to express those functions competently, and the contexts and situations in which the functions and grammar are used. This "tri-dimensional clustering" of function, form, and content is the organizing principle behind each lesson and the cornerstone of the *Communicator* approach to functional syllabus design. *Communicator* offers students broad exposure to uses of language in a variety of relevant contexts: in community, academic, employment, home, and social settings. The text gives students practice using a variety of registers; from the formal language someone might use in a job interview, with a customer, or when speaking to an authority figure; to the informal language someone would use when talking with family members, co-workers, or friends.

A special feature of the course is the treatment of discourse strategies — initiating conversations and topics, interrupting, hesitating, asking for clarification, and other conversation skills.

An Overview

Chapter-Opening Photos

Each chapter-opening page features two photographs of situations that depict key functions presented in the chapter. Students make predictions about who the people are and what they might be saying to each other. In this way, students have the opportunity to share what they already know and to relate the chapter's content to their own lives and experiences.

Guided Conversations

Guided conversations are the dialogs and exercises that are the central learning devices in *Communicator*. Each lesson begins with a model guided conversation that illustrates the use of one or more functions and the structures they require, all in the context of a meaningful exchange of communication. Key functional expressions in the models are in bold-face type and are footnoted, referring students to short lists of alternative expressions for accomplishing the functions. In the exercises that follow, students create new conversations by placing new content into the framework of the model, and by using any of the alternative functional expressions.

Original Student Conversations

Each lesson ends with an open-ended exercise that offers students the opportunity to create and present original conversations based on the functional theme of the lesson and the alternative expressions. Students contribute content based on their experiences, ideas, and imaginations. The ultimate objective of each lesson is to enable students to use functional expressions competently in creating their own original conversations.

Check-Up

This section features a variety of follow-up exercises and activities:

- **Function Check** exercises provide review and reinforcement of functional expressions presented in the chapter.

- **Grammar Check** exercises offer practice with key grammar structures featured in the guided conversation lessons.

- **Listening Exercises** give students intensive listening practice that focuses on functional communication.

- **InterChange** activities provide opportunities for students to relate lesson content to their own lives.

- **InterCultural Connections** activities offer rich opportunities for cross-cultural comparison.

- **In Your Own Words** activities provide opportunities for writing and discussion of important issues presented in the chapter.

- **InterView** activities encourage students to interview each other as well as people in the community.

- **InterAct!** activities provide opportunities for role playing and cooperative learning.

- **Reading** passages in every chapter are designed to provide interesting and stimulating content for class discussion. These selections are also available on the accompanying audiotapes for additional listening comprehension practice.

Communicators

This end-of-chapter activity offers students the opportunity to create and to present "guided role plays." Each activity consists of a model that students can practice and then use as a basis for their original presentations. Students should be encouraged to be inventive and to use new vocabulary in these presentations and should feel free to adapt and expand the model any way they wish.

Scenes & Improvisations

These "free role plays" appear after every third chapter, offering review and synthesis of functions and conversation strategies in the three preceding chapters. Students are presented with eight scenes depicting conversations between people in various situations. The students determine who the people are and what they are talking about, and then improvise based on their perceptions of the scenes' characters, contexts, and situations. These improvisations promote students' absorption of the preceding chapters' functions and strategies into their repertoire of active language use.

Support and Reference Sections

- **End-of-Chapter Summaries** provide complete lists of functional expressions in each chapter.

- A **Notes and Commentary** section in the Appendix provides notes on language usage, grammar, and culture; commentaries on the characters, contexts, and situations; and explanations of idiomatic and colloquial expressions.

- An **Inventory of Functions and Conversation Strategies** in the Appendix offers a comprehensive display of all functional expressions in the text.

- An **Index** provides a convenient reference for locating functions and grammar in the text.

Suggested Teaching Strategies

We encourage you, in using *Communicator*, to develop approaches and strategies that are compatible with your own teaching style and the needs and abilities of your students. While the program does not require any specific method or technique in order to be used effectively, you may find it helpful to review and try out some of the following suggestions. (Specific step-by-step instructions may be found in the *Communicator Teacher's Guide*.)

Chapter-Opening Photos

Have students talk about the people and the situations and, as a class or in pairs, predict what the characters might be saying to each other. Students in pairs or small groups may enjoy practicing role plays based on these scenes and then presenting them to the class.

Guided Conversations

1. LISTENING: With books closed, have students listen to the model conversation — presented by you, by a pair of students, or on the audiotape.

2. DISCUSSION: Have students discuss the model conversation: Who are the people? What is the situation?

    At this point, you should call students' attention to any related Language and Culture Notes, which can be found in the Appendix.

3. READING: Have students follow along as two students present the model with books open.

4. PRACTICE: Have students practice the model conversation in pairs, small groups, or as a class.

5. ALTERNATIVE EXPRESSIONS: Present to the class each sentence of the dialog containing a footnoted expression. Call on different students to present the same sentence, replacing the footnoted expression with its alternatives. (You can cue students to do this quickly by asking, "What's another way of saying that?" or "How else could he/she/you say that?")

6. PAIR PRACTICE (optional): Have pairs of students simultaneously practice all the exercises, using the footnoted expressions or any of their alternatives.

7. PRESENTATION: Call on pairs of students to present the exercises, using the footnoted expressions or any of their alternatives. Before students present, set the scene by describing the characters and the context, or have students do this themselves.

Original Student Conversations

In these activities, which follow the guided conversations at the end of each lesson, have pairs of students create and present original conversations based on the theme of the lesson and any of the alternative expressions. Encourage students to be inventive as they create their characters and situations. (You may want students to prepare their original conversations as homework, then practice them the next day with another student and present them to the class. In that way, students can review the previous day's lesson without actually having to repeat the specific exercises already covered.)

InterChange

Have students first work in pairs and then share with the class what they talked about.

In Your Own Words

This activity is designed for both writing practice and discussion. Have students discuss the activity as a class, in pairs, or in small groups. Then have students write their responses at home, share their written work with other students, and discuss in class. Students may enjoy keeping a journal of their written work. If time permits, you may want to write a response in each student's journal, sharing your own opinions and experiences as well as reacting to what the student has written. If you are keeping portfolios of students' work, these compositions serve as excellent examples of students' progress in learning English.

InterCultural Connections

Have students do the activity as a class, in pairs, or in small groups.

InterView

Have students circulate around the room to conduct their interviews, or have students interview people outside the class. Students should then report back to the class about their interviews.

InterAct!

Have pairs of students practice role-playing the activity and then present their role plays to the class.

Reading

Have students discuss the topic of the reading beforehand, using the pre-reading questions suggested in the *Teacher's Guide*. Have students then read the passage silently, or have them listen to the passage and take notes as you read it or play the audiotape. The *Teacher's Guide* also contains a list of questions designed to check students' comprehension of the passage.

Communicators

Have students practice the model, using the same steps listed above for guided conversations. Then have pairs of students create and present original conversations, using the model dialog as a guide. Encourage students to be inventive and to use new vocabulary. (You may want to assign this exercise as homework, having students prepare their conversations, practice them the next day with another student, and then present them to the class.) Students should present their conversations without referring to the written text, but they should also not memorize them. Rather, they should feel free to adapt and expand them any way they wish.

Scenes & Improvisations

Have students talk about the people and the situations, and then present role plays based on the scenes. Students may refer back to previous lessons as a resource, but they should not simply re-use specific conversations. (You may want to assign these exercises as written homework, having students prepare their conversations, practice them the next day with another student, and then present them to the class.)

In conclusion, we have attempted to offer students a communicative, meaningful, and lively way of practicing the functions of English, along with the grammar structures needed to express them competently. While conveying to you the substance of our textbook, we hope that we have also conveyed the spirit: that learning to communicate in English can be genuinely interactive . . . truly relevant to our students' lives . . . and fun!

Steven J. Molinsky
Bill Bliss

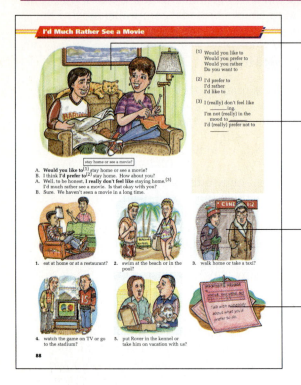

A **model conversation** offers initial practice with the functions and structures of the lesson.

Key functional expressions are in bold-face type and are footnoted, referring students to a box containing alternative expressions for accomplishing the functions.

In the **exercises**, students create conversations by placing new contexts, content, or characters into the model, and by using any of the alternative functional expressions.

The **open-ended exercise** at the end of each lesson asks students to create and present original conversations on the theme of the lesson and any of the alternative expressions.

For example:

Exercise 1 might be completed by placing the new exercise content into the existing model:

A. Would you like to eat at home or at a restaurant?
B. I think I'd prefer to eat at home. How about you?
A. Well, to be honest, I really don't feel like eating at home. I'd much rather eat at a restaurant. Is that okay with you?
B. Sure. We haven't eaten at a restaurant in a long time.

Exercise 2 might be completed by using the new exercise content *and* some of the alternative functional expressions:

A. Would you prefer to swim at the beach or in the pool?
B. I think I'd like to swim at the beach. How about you?
A. Well, to be honest, I'm not really in the mood to swim at the beach. I'd much rather swim in the pool. Is that okay with you?
B. Sure. We haven't swum in the pool in a long time.

Using the Footnotes

1. ( ) indicates that the word or words are optional. For example, the sentence:

   I'm (very) sorry to hear that. = I'm sorry to hear that.
   I'm very sorry to hear that.

2. / indicates that the words on either side of the / mark are interchangeable. For example, the sentence:

   I don't/can't believe it! = I don't believe it!
   I can't believe it!

3. Sometimes the ( ) and / symbols appear together. For example, the sentence:

   I'm not (completely/absolutely) positive. = I'm not positive.
   I'm not completely positive.
   I'm not absolutely positive.

4. Sometimes the footnote indicates that an alternative expression requires a change in the grammar of the sentence. For example, the sentences:

   I don't feel like _____ing. = I don't feel like dancing.
   I'd prefer not to _____. = I'd prefer not to dance.

1 MEETING AND GREETING PEOPLE

Michael and Karen are students at Jefferson High School. They're meeting for the first time. What do you think they're saying to each other?

PEOPLE ARE DRESSING DOWN /TO DRESSED DOWN

Maria Fernandez is introducing David Chen and Tom Wilson to each other at a business meeting. What do you think all three of them are saying?

PEOPLE ARE DRESSED UP

Carmen | Japan / Venezuela | Kenji

(1) My name is
I'm

(2) Hello.

[less formal]
Hi.

[more formal]
How do you do?

(3) (It's) nice to meet you.
(It's) nice meeting you.
(I'm) happy to meet you.
(I'm) glad to meet you.
(I'm) pleased to meet you.
(It's) a pleasure to meet you.

(4) How about you?
What about you?
And you?
greeting = hi = hello = hola

A. I don't think we've met. **My name is**(1) Carmen.
B. **Hello.**(2) **I'm**(1) Kenji. **Nice to meet you.**(3)
A. **Nice meeting you,**(3) too. Tell me, where are you from?
B. Japan. **How about you?**(4)
A. Venezuela.

Tom | Carol

1. dancer
English teacher

Arlene | Betty

2. 2C
4D

Pedro | Nick

3. two months
one year

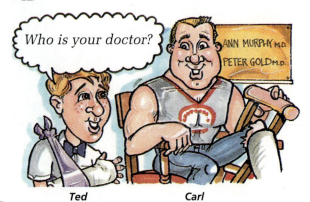

Ted | Carl

4. Dr. Murphy
Dr. Gold

Frank   Gloria

5. Accounting
Shipping

Karen   Bob

6. History
Chemistry

Jane   Sally

7. the morning shift
the night shift

Alan   Ruth

8. the bride's
the groom's

Steve   Judy

9. a lawyer
a journalist

Paul   Dave

10. rock
jazz

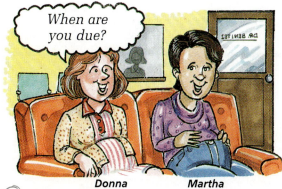

Donna   Martha

11. next month
any day now

Introduce yourself to somebody.

Function Check: *What's My Line?*

Choose the appropriate line for Speaker B.

	A	**B**
1.	I don't think we've met.	a. How about you? ⓑ. How do you do? c. What about you?
2.	My name is Jane.	a. And you? b. Hello. My name is David. c. I'm glad.
3.	Nice to meet you. What do you do?	a. I'm fine, thanks. b. I'm pleased to meet you. c. I'm a lawyer.
4.	I'm from Bogota. What about you?	a. I'm a doctor. b. I'm from Los Angeles. c. I'm happy to meet you.
5.	I'm pleased to meet you.	a. Nice meeting you, too. b. How about you? c. What about you?
6.	I'm a History major. And you?	a. My major is Chemistry. b. Every day. c. I'm a teacher.
7.	I like skiing. What about you?	a. And you? b. I like it, too. c. I'm happy.

Listening: *The Best Response*

Listen and choose the best response.

1. a. Fine, thanks.
   b. All right.
   ⓒ. I'm a lawyer.

2. a. I'm fine.
   b. Nice to meet you.
   c. I'm an engineer.

3. a. New York.
   b. 2D.
   c. Yes, I do.

4. a. I've been studying.
   b. In Taipei.
   c. Two months.

5. a. I'm a student.
   b. Math.
   c. I'm an accountant.

6. a. I like jazz.
   b. Next month.
   c. Yes, I do.

Listening: *Conclusions*

Listen and choose the best conclusion.

1. (a.) John and Paul are old friends.
   b. John and Paul are meeting for the first time.
   c. John asked Paul what time it was.

2. a. They're good friends.
   b. This is the first time they've met.
   c. Sam thinks he's met Dr. Jones before.

3. a. Sally has met Tom before.
   b. Sally and Tom are both happy to meet each other.
   c. Tom thinks Sally is nice.

4. a. Kim wants to go to Spain.
   b. Kim wants to know where Luis is from.
   c. Kim wants to know how Luis is feeling.

5. a. Ruth is going to see Martha.
   b. Ruth is leaving Martha's office.
   c. Martha is asking Ruth where she's going.

Grammar Check: *WH- Questions*

This man is at an employment agency. Complete the interviewer's questions using the appropriate WH- words.

Who	What	Where	When	Why

A. _____ What's your name _____ ?
B. Peter van Dyke.
A. _____, Mr. van Dyke?
B. I'm from Holland.
A. I see. And _____?
B. I'm an illustrator.
A. That's interesting. And _____?
B. At the Leiden Design Company in Amsterdam.
A. Uh-húh. And _____?
B. I decided to move to the United States because I wanted some overseas experience.
A. And _____?
B. I want to start working as soon as possible.
A. Tell me, _____?
B. You can call my previous employer, Mrs. Jensen, for a recommendation.
A. Okay. I'll see what I can do.
B. Thank you very much. I look forward to hearing from you.

InterChange

Talk with a partner about what you do when you first meet someone.

How do you usually start the conversation?
What do you normally ask about?
Do you ever feel shy and nervous when you meet someone for the first time?

Then tell the class what you learned about each other.

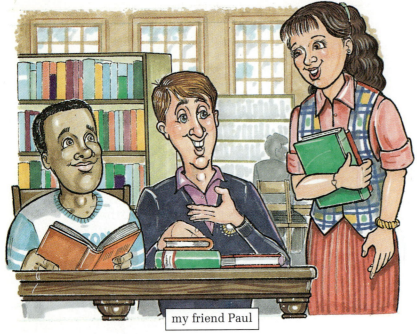

my friend Paul

(1) How are you?
How have you been?

[less formal]
How are you doing?
How are things?
How's it going?

(2) Fine (thank you/thanks).
Good.
All right.
Okay.
Not bad.

(3) Let me introduce (you to)
I'd like to introduce (you to)
I'd like you to meet

[less formal]
Meet
This is

A. Hi! **How are you?**(1)
B. **Fine.**(2) And you?
A. **Fine, thanks.**(2) **Let me introduce you to**(3) my friend Paul.
B. Nice to meet you.

1. my brother Tom

2. my sister Kate

3. my roommate, Peter

4. my English teacher,
Mrs. Simon

5. my fiancé, Steve Smith

Introduce a
friend to
somebody else.

6

(1) Excuse me,
Pardon me,

(2) Sure.
Of course.

(3) I'm sorry.
Excuse me.

A. **Excuse me,**(1) but don't I know you from somewhere?
B. No, I don't think so.
A. **Sure.**(2) Don't you work at the bank on Main Street?
B. No, I'm afraid not. You must have me confused with somebody else.
A. Oh, **I'm sorry.**(3) I guess I made a mistake.

1.

2.

3.

4.

5.

Greet someone you think you recognize.

* Federal Bureau of Investigation

Over the years, Americans have greeted each other in a variety of ways. Many years ago, Native Americans raised one hand as a sign of peace and friendship and said "How!," a greeting from the Sioux language. Early colonists who came to the New World seeking religious freedom often greeted each other with biblical phrases such as "Peace be with you." Other groups brought with them courtly European gestures such as bowing and curtsying. The greater the status of the person greeted, the deeper the bow or curtsy. In informal situations, men shook hands with each other and kissed the hands of women. As time passed, the bow evolved into a simple tip of the hat and the curtsy became a nod of the head. "How do you do?" was shortened to "Howdy," a greeting still heard in some parts of the United States today. In recent times, the handshake has become the common gesture of greeting for both men and women.

When Americans shake hands, they usually stand about two feet apart. If they are friends, they may also pat each other on the shoulder or arm. Women sometimes exchange a kiss on the cheek or a quick hug.

The greeting "Hi, how are you?" has become a routine way of saying hello and is not usually meant as a question about how the other person is feeling. The response "Fine, thanks" is very typical and does not necessarily convey any real information.

Americans consider a firm handshake the trademark of a strong character. People think that many virtues of manhood or womanhood are conveyed in the strength of a handshake and that, conversely, a weak handshake implies a weak character. Americans often form a first impression about people by the way they shake hands.

Choose

1. The way Americans greet each other today depends on _____.
   a. how well they know each other
   b. the early colonists
   c. a firm handshake

2. When people say, "Hi, how are you?" they are usually _____.
   a. asking about someone's health
   b. shaking hands
   c. greeting someone

3. Greetings vary _____.
   a. according to first impressions
   b. through time
   c. about two feet apart

4. People think that the strength of a person's handshake conveys _____.
   a. politeness
   b. virtues and vices
   c. strength of character

Tell about how people greet each other in your country.

Is it common to shake hands? to kiss?
How do men greet each other?
How do women greet each other?

How do men greet women?
How do women greet men?
How do adults greet children?

In Your Own Words

For Writing and Discussion

Our first impressions, our opinions about people the first time we meet them, are important. Different people have different standards for judging others the first time they meet.

Think about the following characteristics. Which do you consider important and which do you consider unimportant when forming an impression of somebody else?

a firm handshake

a confident walk

a humble demeanor

a well-groomed appearance

an honest, open face

good "eye contact"

interesting to talk to

a quiet, serious attitude

an air of self-assurance

attractive features

a sense of humor

a friendly smile

a graduate of an important university

a member of a prominent family

an important person in a company

Tell about a person you feel would make a good first impression.

Kathy Wilson

She saved my life when I almost drowned at the beach last year.

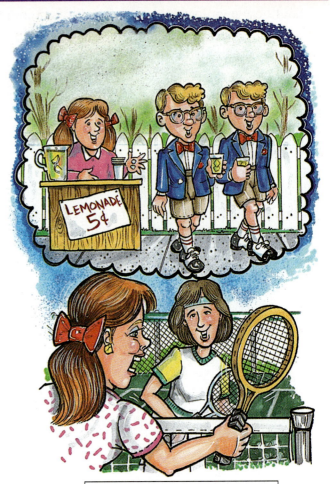

The Bradley twins

Their parents used to dress them alike all the time.

A. **Guess**[1] who I **saw**[2] yesterday!
B. Who?
A. Kathy Wilson!
B. Kathy Wilson? I don't think I remember her.
A. Sure you do! She's the one who saved my life when I almost drowned at the beach last year.
B. Oh, of course. Now I remember her. How IS she?
A. **Pretty good.**[3]
B. Did she have anything to say?
A. Not really. We just talked **for a minute.**[4] But it was really good to see her again.

A. **You won't believe**[1] who I **ran into**[2] yesterday!
B. Who?
A. The Bradley twins!
B. The Bradley twins? I don't think I remember them.
A. Sure you do. They're the ones whose parents used to dress them alike all the time.
B. Oh, of course. Now I remember them. How ARE they?
A. **Fine.**[3]
B. Did they have anything to say?
A. Not really. We just talked **for a moment.**[4] But it was really good to see them again.

[1] Guess	[2] saw	[3] Pretty good.	[4] for a minute
You won't believe	ran into	Fine.	for a moment
	bumped into	Great.	for a few minutes
			for a few seconds

1. Professor Kingston

He taught Economic Theory at Business School.

2. Mr. and Mrs. Larson

They used to live next door to us when we lived across town.

3. Miss Hubbard

Her car would always break down in front of our house.

4. The Bennetts

Their daughter baby-sits for us every once in a while.

5. Lucy Crawford

She's the head of the Board of Education.

6. Patty Taylor

She had a crush on me in sixth grade.

7. Mr. and Mrs. Miller

They're retired and living in Florida now.

8. Eddie Long

He was my high school sweetheart.

9. Butch Baker

His dog would always get loose and scare all the children in the neighborhood.

Tell a friend about somebody you saw yesterday.

Function Check: *What's the Expression?*

Choose the appropriate line for Speaker A.

	A	**B**
1.	(a.) How's it going? b. Don't I know you from somewhere? c. Did she have anything to say?	All right.
2.	a. I guess I made a mistake. b. I don't think I remember her. c. We just talked for a minute.	Oh, sure you do!
3.	a. It was really good to see you again. b. Now I remember her. c. You must have me confused with somebody else.	Excuse me.
4.	a. How are you? b. Guess who I saw yesterday! c. Oh, sure you do!	Who?
5.	a. Of course. b. Let me introduce you to my friend Susan. c. Don't I know you from somewhere?	No, I don't think so.
6.	a. Did they have anything to say? b. We just talked for a minute. c. They don't look very well.	Not really.

Grammar Check: *Verb Tenses*

1. I _____ my cousin for lunch today.
 a. meet
 (b.) met
 c. would meet

2. I _____ him every once in a while.
 a. was running into
 b. am running into
 c. run into

3. David _____ in San Francisco when he was younger.
 a. lives
 b. is living
 c. used to live

4. _____ a good time at the party?
 a. Had you
 b. Did you have
 c. Haven't you

5. Where _____ after the lecture?
 a. you went
 b. were you go
 c. did you go

6. Who _____ the head of the department?
 a. does
 b. is
 c. be

Grammar Check: *Relative Pronouns*

Alan works at the post office.	A. Who is Alan? B. He's *the one who* works at the post office.
Bob's wife works at the bank.	A. Who is Bob? B. He's *the one whose* wife works at the bank.
Tim and Susan live in Toronto.	A. Who are Tim and Susan? B. They're *the ones who* live in Toronto.
This house has a yellow door.	A. Which house is this? B. It's *the one that* has a yellow door.

Choose the correct "one."

a. the one who	c. the one that	e. the one whose
b. the ones who	d. the ones that	f. the ones whose

a 1. Ernest Hemingway was a famous author. He was _____ wrote *The Sun Also Rises*.

_____ 2. Thomas Edison was an inventor. He was _____ creative ideas led to the invention of the light bulb.

_____ 3. Degas, Monet, and Renoir were French artists. They were some of _____ began the movement called Impressionism.

_____ 4. Beethoven was a German composer. He was _____ composed "Für Elise."

_____ 5. Albert Einstein was a physicist. His theories were _____ explained the idea of gravitational forces.

_____ 6. Sally Ride was an astronaut. She was _____ flight made history because she was the first American woman to travel in space.

_____ 7. Abraham Lincoln was a U.S. president. He was _____ freed the slaves.

_____ 8. "Peanuts" is a comic strip. It is _____ has a round-faced boy named Charlie Brown and his dog, Snoopy.

_____ 9. Romeo and Juliet are famous Shakespearean characters. They're _____ parents disapproved of their love.

InterAct!

Role Play: *Guess Who YOU Saw Yesterday!*

YOU'RE the one who ran into one of the characters on pages 10 or 11! Was it Kathy Wilson, Professor Kingston, Butch Baker, or perhaps the Bradley twins? You decide, and then with a partner create a conversation and present it to the class.

SUMMARY

Here are the expressions you practiced in Chapter 1. Try to use as many as you can to expand your vocabulary and to add variety to your use of English.

Greeting People

Hello.

[less formal]
Hi.

[more formal]
How do you do?

(It's) nice to meet you.
(It's) nice meeting you.
(I'm) happy to meet you.
(I'm) glad to meet you.
(I'm) pleased to meet you.

How are you?
How have you been?
[less formal]
How are you doing?
How are things?
How's it going?
    Fine (thank you/thanks).
    Good.
    All right.
    Okay.
    Not bad.

Introductions

Introducing Oneself

My name is _____.
I'm _____.

Introducing Others

Let me introduce (you to) _____.
I'd like to introduce (you to) _____.
I'd like you to meet _____.
[less formal]
Meet _____.
This is _____.

Initiating Conversations

I don't think we've met.

Excuse me, but . . .
Pardon me, but . . .

Don't I know you from somewhere?

Initiating a Topic

Tell me, . . .

Guess _____!
You won't believe _____!

Identifying

My friend *Paul*, my brother *Tom* . . .

She's the one who _____.

Apologizing

I'm sorry.
Excuse me.

Asking for and Reporting Information

Where are you from?
    Japan.
What do you do?
    I'm an *English teacher.*
Which *apartment do you live in?*
How long *have you been studying here?*
Who *is your doctor?*
Whose *family are you in?*
What kind of *music do you play?*
When *are you due?*

How about you?
What about you?
And you?

Don't you work at the bank on Main Street?

How is she?
    Pretty good.
    Fine.
    Great.

Did _____ have anything to say?

2

SHARING NEWS AND INFORMATION
DESCRIBING PEOPLE

David has just received a letter with some good news, and he's sharing the news with his co-worker, Brenda. What do you think they're saying to each other?

Kevin and Allison are talking about their teacher. What do you think they're saying?

promoted to assistant manager

A. I have some good news.
B. Really? What is it?
A. I was just promoted to assistant manager!
B. Assistant manager?! **That's fantastic!**[1] You must be **thrilled.**[2]
A. I am.
B. Congratulations! **I'm very happy to hear that.**[3]
A. Thanks.

[1] That's fantastic!
That's great!
That's wonderful!
That's exciting!
That's marvelous!

[2] thrilled
excited
very pleased
ecstatic

[3] I'm very happy to
hear that.
I'm very happy for you.

1. given a 20 percent raise

2. accepted at Oxford University

3. awarded the Nobel Prize for Physics

4. named "Employee of the Year"

5. offered a movie contract by a major Hollywood studio

Share some good news with a friend.

My husband just lost his job.

A. I have some bad news.
B. Oh? What is it?
A. My husband just lost his job.
B. He did?
A. I'm afraid so.
B. **That's too bad!**(1) You must be very upset.
A. I am.
B. **I'm very sorry to hear about that.**(2)

(1) That's too bad!
That's a shame!
That's a pity!
What a shame!
What a pity!

(2) I'm (very) sorry to hear about that.
I'm (very) sorry.
I'm so sorry.

1. My dog was run over by a car.

2. The factory where I work is going to shut down next month.

3. My son and his wife have decided to get a divorce.

4. I have to stay home all weekend and take care of my little brother.

5. I was rejected by every medical school I applied to.

The National Star

Share some bad news with a friend.

17

Grammar Check: *Passives*

Turn the following sentences into the passive.

IBM just offered me a job.
I was just offered a job by IBM.

1. My father built that house.
2. A famous chef is preparing food for the visiting diplomats.
3. The principal makes announcements every Monday morning.
4. The National Science Foundation is going to give Janet a grant to do research.
5. Vincent van Gogh painted that painting.
6. The President had signed the bill just before he left office.
7. A wonderful florist will decorate the church.
8. Christian Dior has designed my wedding dress.

Listening: *What's the Meaning?*

Listen and choose the answer that is closest in meaning to the sentence you have heard.

1. a. The news was good today.
   b. I have something good to tell you.
   c. I have something new to tell you.

2. a. Are you sick?
   b. I'm sure you're happy.
   c. That's too bad.

3. a. What happened?
   b. I'm happy for you.
   c. I didn't hear that.

4. a. That's wonderful!
   b. What a pity!
   c. That's a shame!

5. a. That's too bad.
   b. I forgive you.
   c. I didn't hear that.

6. a. You must be thrilled.
   b. You must sit up.
   c. I think you're unhappy about that.

Listening: *The Best Response*

Listen and choose the best response.

1. a. Oh? What is it?
   b. Well, congratulations!
   c. That's fantastic!

2. a. Oh, that's a pity!
   b. Really? What a shame!
   c. Really? Congratulations!

3. a. Oh, I'm sorry to hear that.
   b. What a thrill!
   c. I'm so pleased!

4. a. What a shame!
   b. That's exciting!
   c. I'm sorry to hear that.

5. a. Oh, that's too bad!
   b. I'm very happy to hear that.
   c. You must be ecstatic!

6. a. That's exciting!
   b. I'm very pleased.
   c. That's a shame.

7. a. I'm thrilled for you.
   b. I'm very sorry.
   c. You did?

8. a. You must be thrilled.
   b. I'm afraid so.
   c. That's terrible!

Grammar Check: *Deductions with MUST*

Decide which descriptive adjective is most appropriate.

patient	intelligent	honest
strict	short-tempered	sick
articulate	upset	lonely

1. A. The babysitter spent three hours trying to get the baby to stop crying.

    B. *She must be very patient.*

2. A. Mrs. Lyman wrote a brilliant analysis of the problem.

    B. _____

3. A. Simon was rushed to the hospital early this morning!

    B. _____

4. A. Mr. Wilson wouldn't let his class leave until exactly 3:00 P.M.

    B. _____

5. A. I used to live with three roommates, but they all moved out.

    B. _____

6. A. My cousin George fights with people all the time!

    B. _____

7. A. The president spoke clearly and concisely. She gave an excellent speech!

    B. _____

8. A. Jennifer found a twenty-dollar bill and took it to the police right away.

    B. _____

9.

My cat ran away!

For Writing and Discussion

We've all experienced *highs* and *lows* in our lives—times when good things have happened and times when bad things have happened. Share with other students in your class some of the good things and some of the bad things that have happened to you. Of course, everybody will react with the appropriate *good news* or *bad news* responses!

That's fantastic!   *What a shame!*   *I'm so sorry.*   *I'm happy to hear that.*

your granddaughter

your cousin Ralph

A. Have you **heard from**[1] your granddaughter lately?
B. As a matter of fact, I have. I **heard from**[1] her just the other day.
A. **How's she doing?**[2]
B. **Fine.**[3] She's getting straight A's in school.
A. That's fantastic!
B. I think so, too.
A. Next time you see her, please **give her my regards.**[4]
B. I will.

A. Have you **run into**[1] your cousin Ralph lately?
B. As a matter of fact, I have. I **ran into**[1] him just the other day.
A. **How's he doing?**[2]
B. **Not too well.**[5] He had to have four teeth pulled last week.
A. That's too bad!
B. I think so, too.
A. Next time you see him, please **tell him I'm thinking of him.**[4]
B. I will.

[1] heard from	[2] How's *she* doing?	[4] give *her* my regards	[5] Not too well.
run into	How is *she*?	tell *her* I said hello	Not so well.
talked to	How has *she* been?	tell *her* I'm	Not very well.
seen		thinking of *her*	
spoken to	[3] Fine.		
been in touch with	Great.		
	Wonderful.		

1. your parents

2. your neighbors across the street

3. your son

4. your cousins in Detroit

5. George and Irene

6. Janet

7. your friend Elizabeth

8. your grandfather

9. the president

* Parent Teacher Association

Grammar Check: *Verb Tenses*

A

1. Have you _____ your cousin Betty recently?
   a. seen ⟨circled⟩
   b. been
   c. talked

3. How _____ she?
   a. is doing
   b. has been
   c. is

5. That's too _____.
   a. pity
   b. bad
   c. great

7. Oh. How _____ he been?
   a. has
   b. is
   c. was

9. That's _____!
   a. fantastic
   b. ecstatic
   c. well

11. How _____?
    a. has he done
    b. is he doing
    c. was he doing

13. That's great. Next time you _____ him, send him my regards.
    a. see
    b. saw
    c. will see

B

2. Yes. I _____ her the other day.
   a. been in touch with
   b. ran into
   c. seen

4. She's not _____.
   a. lately
   b. very
   c. well

6. Incidentally, I _____ your Uncle Harry the other day.
   a. saw
   b. talked
   c. hear from

8. He _____.
   a. wonderful
   b. has been all right
   c. fine

10. Oh. Before I forget, I _____ from my brother Bill yesterday.
    a. was hearing
    b. have heard
    c. heard

12. He's fine. He _____ a new law firm last month.
    a. is joining
    b. has joining
    c. joined

14. _____ to do that.
    a. I'm sure
    b. I'll be sure
    c. Are you sure

For Writing and Discussion

Who are the people you keep in touch with on a regular basis? How often do you speak to them? What do you usually talk about?

Tell about some people you would *like to* hear from more often.

You Won't Believe Who I Ran Into!

Think of some famous people. For example:

a famous actor or actress

a famous sports star

a famous rock star

a famous musician

a famous dancer

a famous politician

Think of a few things you know about each of these people.

. . . .

. . . .

. . . .

. . . .

. . . .

. . . .

With a partner, tell about conversations you had with these famous people you recently ran into. Tell what you talked about, but don't tell the people's names! See if your partner can guess who they are.

Then practice some of these conversations with your partner, present them to the class, and see if others can guess who your famous friends are!

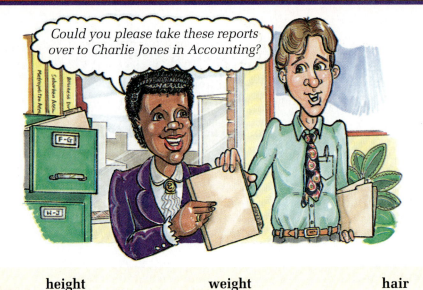

A. Could you please take these reports over to Charlie Jones in Accounting?

B. Sure. I'd be happy to. But I'm afraid I don't remember what he looks like.

A. You can't miss him. He's **about your height, sort of heavy**, with **curly dark** hair.

B. Okay. I think I'll be able to find him.

A. Thanks very much. I appreciate it.

height	weight	hair		additional features
about your height	sort of ⎫	curly	dark	and (wears) glasses
about average height	kind of ⎬ heavy/thin	wavy	light	and (has) a beard/
about ____ feet tall	very ⎭	straight	brown	mustache
(very) tall	a little on the heavy		black	
(very) short	side		blond(e)	
a little taller/shorter			red	
than you/me			gray	

Complete these conversations using the information above.

1. Could you please take these boxes over to Stella in Shipping?

2. Would you be willing to pick up Mr. Hamilton at the airport?

3. Could you possibly get some chalk from Ms. Crenshaw in the principal's office?

4. Could I possibly ask you to meet my sister at the train station?

5. Could I possibly ask you to take another picture of my Uncle Harry?

Talk with somebody about what another person looks like.

What Are They Like?

our new English teacher
intelligent
patient

(1) Have you heard anything
     Do you know anything

(2) People say
     They say
     People tell me
     Everybody says
     Everybody tells me
     I've heard
     Word has it (that)

(3) What else have you
        heard?
     Have you heard anything
        else?
     Do you know anything
        else?

A. **Have you heard anything**(1) about our new English teacher?
B. Yes. **People say**(2) she's very intelligent.
A. **What else have you heard?**(3)
B. Well, they also say she's very patient.
A. Really? That's interesting.

1. the new boss
   bright
   strict

2. the new superintendent
   friendly
   helpful

3. the new student in our class
   nice
   outgoing

4. our new senator
   articulate
   honest

5. the new supervisor
   unfriendly
   short-tempered

Talk with a friend about what somebody is like.

25

Vocabulary Check: *"Out of Place"*

Which word does not relate to the rest of the words in the group?

1. height: (a.) long   b. short   c. tall   d. average
2. weight: a. thin   b. heavy   c. fat   d. thick
3. hair: a. curly   b. wavy   c. heavy   d. straight
4. hair color: a. black   b. blond   c. gray   d. yellow
5. additional features: a. beard   b. glasses   c. watch   d. mustache

Grammar Check: *AND and BUT*

Choose the correct word.

1. A. Have you heard anything about our new science teacher?
   B. Yes. People say she's patient ((and)   but) kind.

2. A. What have you heard about our new history teacher?
   B. Everybody tells me she's nice (and   but) boring.

3. A. What have you heard about the new supervisor?
   B. They say he's intelligent (and   but) not very friendly.

4. A. Have you heard anything else about him?
   B. Well, word has it that he's short-tempered (and but) inconsiderate.

5. A. Do you know anything about Linda's new boyfriend?
   B. Yes. Everybody tells me he's interesting (and   but) conceited.

6. A. What have you heard about the new Walt Disney film?
   B. People say it's educational (and   but) enjoyable.

7. A. What have you heard about our new boss?
   B. They say he's friendly (and   but) helpful.
   A. Well, I've heard that he's very aggressive (and   but) nice.

8.

I've heard that the new kid up the block is mean (and   but) selfish.

Everybody at school tells me that he's lazy (and   but) inconsiderate!

"Mystery Person"

Describe someone to your partner. Tell what the person looks like and what the person is like, but don't give the person's name. See if your partner can guess who you're describing. Then give your descriptions to the class and see if they can guess who the "mystery person" is!

"Missing Person"

Half the students in the class are "police officers." The other students are very upset. A friend or family member is missing! These people go to the police to report the missing person. The police have to complete the following *Missing Person Report* by asking the questions on the form.

MISSING PERSON REPORT

Name of missing person _____

Age _____ Height _____ Hair _____ Eyes _____ Weight _____

Address of missing person _____

Personal Information:

Married: yes _____ no _____

Children: yes _____ no _____

Date last seen _____ Where _____

Possible reasons for disappearing:

	YES	NO
Problems at work	___	___
Problems at home	___	___
Health problems	___	___

Explain _____

PERSON REPORTING THE MISSING PERSON

Relation to missing person _____

Name _____

Address _____

Telephone number _____

Is the person reporting
1) upset?
2) nervous?
3) indifferent?
4) sad?
5) happy?

Date filed: _____

Officer's signature: _____

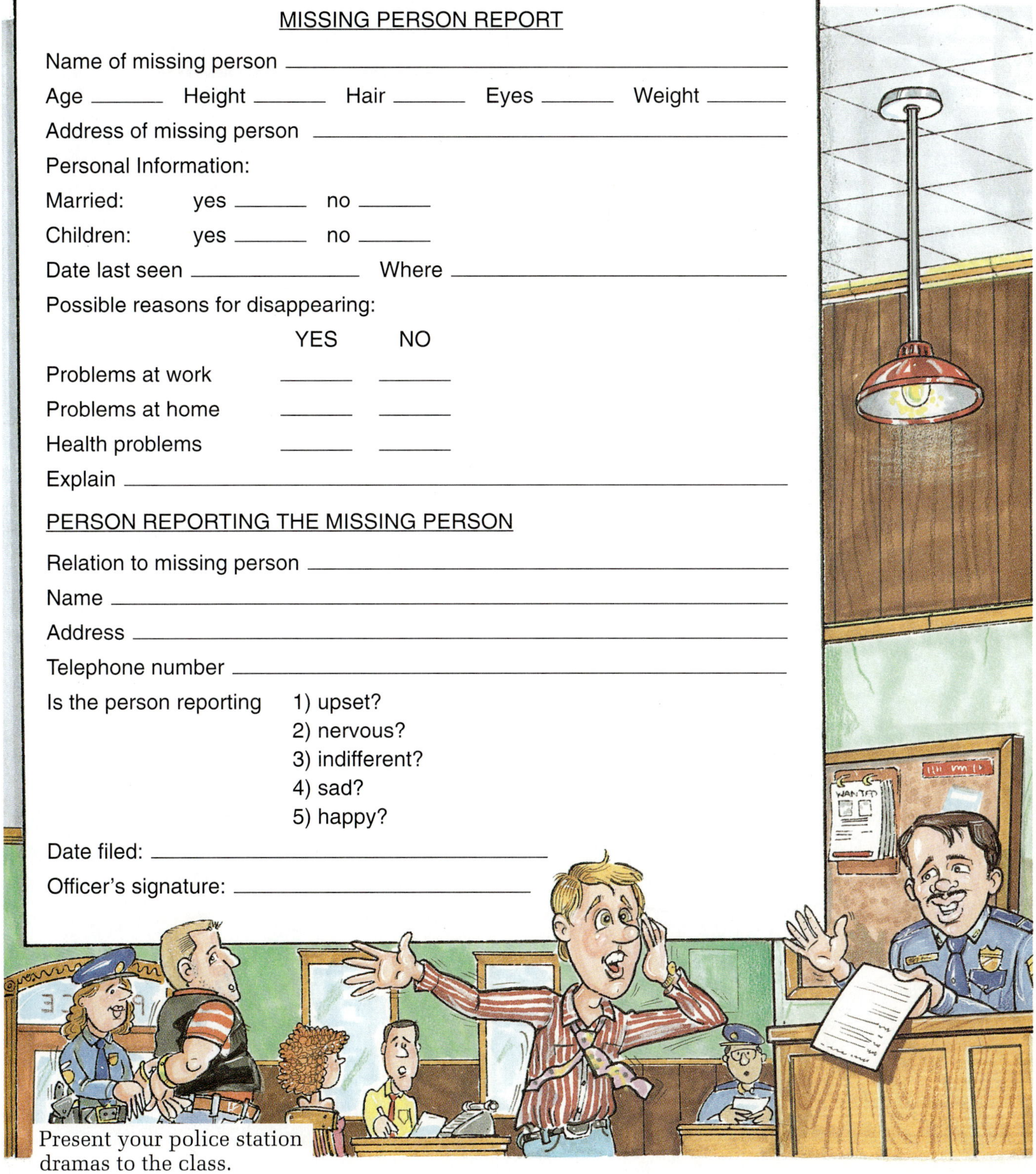

Present your police station dramas to the class.

A. So, tell me a little about yourself.
B. Gee – uh . . . **I don't know where to begin.**(1) **What do you want to know?**(2)
A. Well, let's see . . . What do you do?
B. I'm a civil engineer.
A. Hmm. That's interesting. Do you enjoy your work?
B. Yes. I like it a lot.
A. Tell me, what exactly do you do as a civil engineer?
B. I design roads and bridges for the city.
A. That sounds like a very **exciting**(3) job.
B. It is.

(1) I don't know where to begin.
I don't know where to start.
I don't know what to say.

(2) What do you want to know?
What would you like to know?
What can I tell you?

(3) exciting
interesting
challenging
difficult
important
creative

1.

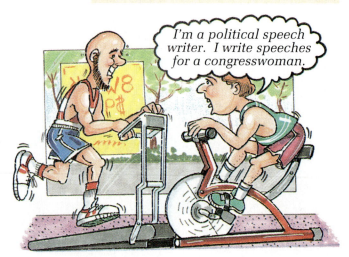

2.

Vocabulary Check: *The Correct Word*

Choose the most appropriate adjective.

1. The ((confused) confusing) meteorologist gave the wrong forecast.

2. Designing roads and bridges is an (excited exciting) job.

3. The ambulance driver was (tired tiring) after a busy night at the hospital.

4. Living among people of other countries is a (fascinated fascinating) experience.

5. Criminal law is an (interested interesting) aspect of our legal system.

6. The real estate agent's monthly sales were (disappointed disappointing).

7. Graphic design is a (challenged challenging) new field in the area of computers.

8. The congressman was (surprised surprising) at the ability of his young speech writer.

9. A forest ranger's work, although quiet, is never (bored boring).

10. The guests at our party were not (amused amusing) by Uncle Charlie's jokes.

Reading: *Meeting People*

When you meet people for the first time, there are certain questions you can safely ask them. In the United States, for example, questions about the kind of work you do, your place of work, and your position at work are perfectly acceptable. In some countries, however, they are considered inappropriate.

Questions about your hobbies, where you live, and what kind of house you live in are also conversation starters in the United States. But in other parts of the world, they are thought of as too personal, as are questions about a person's religious, political, or ethical beliefs. While these are not the first questions you should ask an American, they would not be considered impolite after you've spoken to someone for a while.

Some taboo topics of discussion in many countries include asking how much people earn, how old they are, and how much they have paid for particular items. In general, safe topics are those that deal with generalities such as weather or current events.

Did You Understand?

1. You should (always (never)) ask about a person's salary.
2. In the United States, people often talk about (religion   work) when they first meet someone.
3. "Taboo" means (safe   forbidden).
4. In the United States, people (rarely   usually) ask about a person's position in a company.
5. Questions about (age   the weather) are generally safe topics.

Appropriate or Inappropriate?

Talk with a partner and decide whether the following questions would be appropriate or inappropriate when first meeting someone in the United States. Then discuss what would be appropriate in your country.

Here are the expressions you practiced in Chapter 2. Try to use as many as you can to expand your vocabulary and to add variety to your use of English.

Asking for and Reporting Information

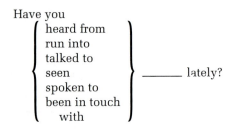

Have you
- heard from
- run into
- talked to
- seen
- spoken to
- been in touch with

_____ lately?

How's _____ doing?
How is _____?
How has _____ been?
   Fine.
   Great.
   Wonderful.
   Not too well.
   Not so well.
   Not very well.

Have you heard anything about _____?
Do you know anything about _____?

People say . . .
They say . . .
People tell me . . .
Everybody says . . .
Everybody tells me . . .
I've heard . . .
Word has it (that) . . .

Tell me a little about yourself.

What do you want to know?
What would you like to know?
What can I tell you?

Asking for and Reporting Additional Information

What else have you heard?
Have you heard anything else?
Do you know anything else?

Initiating a Topic

I have some good/bad news.

Describing

He's about your height, sort of heavy, with curly dark hair.

He's/She's very _____.

Congratulating

That's fantastic!
That's great!
That's wonderful!
That's exciting!
That's marvelous!

Congratulations!

I'm very happy to hear that.
I'm very happy for you.

Sympathizing

That's too bad!
That's a shame!
That's a pity!
What a shame!
What a pity!

I'm (very) sorry to hear about that.
I'm (very) sorry.
I'm so sorry.

Hesitating

Gee-uh . . .

I don't know where to begin.
I don't know where to start.
I don't know what to say.

Well, let's see . . .

Requests

Direct, More Polite

Could you please _____?
Could you possibly _____?
Could I possibly ask you to _____?
Would you be willing to _____?

Surprise-Disbelief

Assistant manager?!

Deduction

You must be _____.

3

DESCRIBING THINGS AND PLACES
REPORTING INFORMATION
REMEMBERING AND FORGETTING

Peter is planning a vacation to a place that Yolanda has visited. What do you think they're saying to each other as they have lunch in the employee cafeteria?

Roy and Diane have just realized they have forgotten to buy an important ingredient for tonight's dinner. What do you think they're saying to each other?

(1) Don't you remember?
You remember.

You should wear your new tie with that jacket.

The children gave you a *blue* tie *with gray and yellow stripes.*

A. You should wear your new tie with that jacket.
B. Which one?
A. The one the children gave you.
B. Hmm. Which one is that?
A. **Don't you remember?**(1) It's the *blue* one *with gray and yellow stripes.*
B. Oh, that one. I know where it is. I'll get it.

Why don't you wear your new bathing suit to the beach?

1. I gave you a *purple* bathing suit *with yellow polka dots.*

How about wearing your new sweater this evening?

2. Aunt Margaret sent you a *wool* sweater *made in Scotland.*

You should wear that pretty scarf of yours.

3. The people at the office gave you a *red* scarf *made of silk.*

Let's take the camera with us!

4. Uncle Harry gave us a *pocket-size* camera *in a brown leather case.*

Why don't you play with your new doll?

5. Grandma sent you a *cute* doll *that cries when you pull the string.*

Remind somebody about a piece of clothing or other item.

Function Check: *Descriptions*

Tom is going on his first business trip, and he's asking his wife for suggestions about what he should pack for the trip.

A. Which suit do you think I should take?

B. I'd take <u>the blue one with black stripes</u> [1].
     (blue/black stripes)

A. Good idea! I should also take a sports jacket. Which one do you think looks best on me?

B. How about _____ [2]?
     (dark brown/I gave you for your birthday)

A. Okay. I'll also need to take along a few ties. Any suggestions?

B. I'd take _____ [3] and
     (red/white dots)

_____ [4].
(yellow/we bought last month)

A. Good! I like those! And what about a camera? Which one should I take?

B. Why don't you take _____ [5]?
     (automatic/black leather case)

A. Great idea! Thanks. I couldn't have packed without you!

Listening: *Where Are They?*

Listen and decide where each conversation is taking place.

1. a. at someone's home
    b. in Scotland
    c. in a department store

2. a. in an office
    b. at someone's home
    c. in a department store

3. a. at a formal party
    b. at someone's home
    c. in a department store

4. a. in a supermarket
    b. in a camera shop
    c. in a leather shop

5. a. in a restaurant
    b. at the beach
    c. at the United Nations

6. a. at Aunt Helen's house
    b. in a restaurant
    c. at someone's home

InterChange

My Favorite Things

Tell about some of your favorite possessions. Where did you get them, and why are they your favorites?

exciting
cool
interesting

(1) As a matter of fact,
In fact,

(2) Can you tell me anything else?
Can you tell me anything more?
What else can you tell me?

(3) in my opinion,
if you ask me,
as far as I'm concerned,

A. Have you by any chance ever been to Tokyo?
B. Yes, I have. Why?
A. I'm going there with my family for a vacation next month. Can you tell me what it's like there?
B. Well, it's a very exciting place. **As a matter of fact,**(1) it's probably one of the most exciting places I know.
A. Really? That's good to hear. **Can you tell me anything else?**(2)
B. Well-uh . . . what else would you like to know?
A. How about the weather . . . and the people?
B. The weather at this time of year is usually cool, and **in my opinion,**(3) the people there are very interesting.
A. It sounds like a wonderful place.
B. It is. I'm sure you'll have a good time there.

1. dynamic
warm
nice

2. nice
pleasant
easygoing

3. pretty
delightful
pleasant

4. charming
cool
helpful

5. lively
comfortable
friendly

Describe a place to a friend.

Listening: *What's the Meaning?*

Listen and choose the answer that is closest in meaning to the sentence you have heard.

1. a. Can you tell me where Kyoto is?
    b. Can you tell me why you like Kyoto?
    c. Can you describe Kyoto?

2. a. I don't know most of the exciting places.
    b. I know many exciting places, but this is more exciting than most.
    c. You know most of the exciting places.

3. a. Did you tell me anything else?
    b. What can you tell me?
    c. Do you know anything else?

4. a. Do you know Elsa?
    b. What other information interests you?
    c. Do you know anything else?

5. a. How are the people at the beaches feeling?
    b. What are the beaches and the people like?
    c. What do the people do at the beaches?

6. a. I'm sure you'll have a great time.
    b. I'm concerned it won't be far enough away.
    c. I'm worried you won't have a good time there.

7. a. I think your china is beautiful.
    b. I believe China is a very pretty country.
    c. I think you should visit China.

8. a. There's something the matter with you.
    b. I think you're correct.
    c. I don't believe you're right.

9. a. He asked me if the people were very friendly.
    b. You asked me if the people were very friendly.
    c. I think the people are very friendly.

InterView

Talk with five people about their favorite places. Ask them to describe these places and tell why they like them. Write down the key descriptive words they use.

Report back to the class and create a summary of *favorite places around the world.*

InterAct!

At the Travel Agency

You can't decide where you and your family will go for a vacation. You go to a travel agent, who has a lot of excellent suggestions about different places to visit.

Role play the scene with another student and then present it to the class.

A. **Do you by any chance know**(1) when the president is going to arrive?
B. Yes. As far as I know, he's going to arrive at 2:30.
A. Hmm. Somehow I thought he was going to arrive earlier than that.
B. **I don't think so.**(2)
A. **Are you sure?**(3)
B. Yes, **I'm positive.**(4) He arrives at 2:30.

1. at nine

2. at four

3. at seven forty-five

4. late next month

5. two weeks from Sunday

Ask somebody for some information.

Grammar Check: *Embedded Questions*

Choose the best answer.

1. Did you tell the taxi driver _____?
   a. where do you want to go
   b. where you wanted to go
   c. where did you want to go

2. Do you remember _____?
   a. what time begins the play
   b. what time does the play begin
   c. what time the play begins

3. Will you ask Mr. Talbot _____?
   a. when should I meet him
   b. when I should meet him
   c. when meet him should I

4. Do you understand _____?
   a. how works the machine
   b. how does the machine work
   c. how the machine works

5. Do you know anyone _____?
   a. who fixes bicycles
   b. who does fix bicycles
   c. who fix bicycles

6. Have you asked the boss _____?
   a. when is she going away
   b. when she going away
   c. when she's going away

7. Do you by any chance know _____?
   a. who is the owner of the store
   b. who the owner is of the store
   c. who the owner of the store is

8. Do you ever wonder _____?
   a. when things will change
   b. when will things chance
   c. when do things change

9.
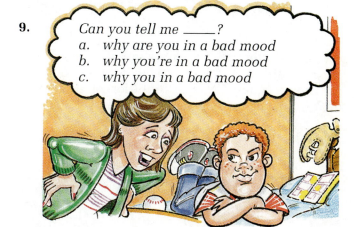

Can you tell me _____?
   a. *why are you in a bad mood*
   b. *why you're in a bad mood*
   c. *why you in a bad mood*

InterChange

Optimists and Pessimists

Some people are optimists. They're always sure that things will turn out well.

I'm sure everybody will have a great time at my party this Saturday!

I'm certain my boss will give me a raise this year! There's no doubt about it!

Other people are pessimists. They're certain that things will turn out badly.

I'm sure it's going to rain at our picnic this weekend. I'm a hundred percent sure!

I know I'm going to flunk my English test tomorrow. I'm absolutely certain!

Think of some things you're *absolutely sure of*. Tell your partner and then the class, and have everybody decide whether you're an optimist or a pessimist.

feed the dog

(1) Did you remember to
_____?
Did you happen to
remember to _____?
You didn't remember to
_____, did you?
You didn't by any chance
remember to _____,
did you?

(2) I forgot (all about it).
I completely forgot.
It (completely) slipped
my mind.

A. Uh-oh! **Did you remember to**(1) feed the dog?
B. No, I didn't. I thought YOU were going to feed him!
A. Hmm. I guess I WAS . . . but **I forgot all about it.**(2)
B. Well, since the dog hasn't been fed yet, I guess one of us should go and do it.
A. Okay. I'll do it.

1. take the garbage out

2. set the table

3. turn the downstairs lights off

4. do the laundry

5. change the baby's diaper

Talk with somebody about something you forgot to do.

Grammar Check: *Sequence of Tenses*

Read each direct quote. Then choose the statement that best reports what the person said.

1. *The movie is terrible!*

   a. I thought the movie is terrible.
   ⓑ I thought the movie was terrible.
   c. I thought this is a terrible movie.

2. *Everything will be fine!*

   a. The police assured me everything will be fine.
   b. The police assured me everything had been fine.
   c. The police assured me everything would be fine.

3. *I didn't finish my homework.*

   a. Tom admitted he didn't finished his homework.
   b. Tom admitted he hadn't finished his homework.
   c. Tom admitted he didn't finish his homework.

4. *I can work late tonight.*

   a. Sally said she worked late tonight.
   b. Sally said she could work late tonight.
   c. Sally said she can work late tonight.

5. *We're telling the truth.*

   a. I knew were they telling the truth.
   b. I knew they are telling the truth.
   c. I knew they were telling the truth.

InterAct!

Absent-Minded People!

Some people are absent-minded. They sometimes forget to do things.

 *I forgot all about it!*

 *It completely slipped my mind!*

With a partner, think of a place. For example:

an office

a restaurant

an auto garage

Decide who the characters in these places are. For example:

*a secretary
a boss*

*a waiter
a cook*

*a customer
a garage mechanic*

One of the people in each of these places is absent-minded. You decide, then create a role play and present it to the class.

School is going to be closed tomorrow!

I heard it on the radio.

A. Did you hear that school is going to be closed tomorrow?
B. **You're kidding!**[1] School isn't really going to be closed tomorrow, is it?
A. Yes, it is.
B. Are you sure?
A. I'm absolutely positive! I heard it on the radio.

1. I saw it in the paper.

They predict a hurricane for tomorrow!

2. I heard it on TV.

We won five gold medals at the Olympics today!

3. I heard it on the radio.

4. I read it in the morning paper.

The Americans and the Europeans have just signed a new trade agreement!

5. I heard it on the 7 o'clock news.

Share some information with a friend.

(1) Where did you hear that?
How do you know (that)?
Who told you (that)?

(2) I don't know for sure.
I'm not (completely) positive.
I'm not absolutely positive.
I'm not a hundred percent positive.

A. Have you heard the news?
B. No, what?
A. They're going to make the park across the street into a parking lot.
B. They're going to make the park across the street into a parking lot?! I don't believe it! **Where did you hear that?**(1)
A. All the neighbors are talking about it.
B. Do you think it's true?
A. I think so, but **I don't know for sure.**(2)
B. Well, personally, I doubt it.

1. It's a rumor going around town.

2. I heard it from some people at the supermarket.

3. I overheard some people talking on the bus.

4. It's a rumor going around the office.

5. Some kids in my class were talking about it.

Share some incredible news with a friend.

43

Grammar Check: *Tag Questions*

Complete the following with tag questions.

1. He can't go, _can he_ ?
2. You aren't Peter Smith, _____?
3. Susan isn't sick again, _____?
4. You're kidding, _____?
5. They've been here before, _____?
6. You'll take care of that, _____?
7. We haven't gone too far, _____?
8. I can leave early, _____?
9. We didn't have any homework, _____?
10. The office is going to be closed tomorrow, _____?
11. You won't be late, _____?

Function Check: *What's My Line?*

Choose the appropriate line for Speaker B.

	A	B
1.	John's getting married!	a. You've got to believe it! b. That can't be it! c.⃝ You've got to be kidding!
2.	Do you think it's true?	a. I'm absolutely positive. b. I can't know for sure. c. I'm completely kidding.
3.	They're making the parking lot into a park.	a. How do you know that? b. I don't know. c. I'm positively.
4.	The president is resigning!	a. No believing! b. Oh, come on! c. When can you hear that?
5.	There's going to be a hurricane tonight!	a. Don't you know for sure? b. Are you positively? c. That can't be!

Listening: *Surprised or Not Surprised?*

Listen and decide according to the intonation whether or not the speaker is surprised.

1. a.⃝ surprised / b. not surprised
2. a. surprised / b. not surprised
3. a. surprised / b. not surprised
4. a. surprised / b. not surprised
5. a. surprised / b. not surprised
6. a. surprised / b. not surprised
7. a. surprised / b. not surprised
8. a. surprised / b. not surprised
9. a. surprised / b. not surprised

Before Johann Gutenberg developed the printing press in 1437, news traveled by word of mouth. This meant that information was slow to reach the public and that details changed as news spread from one person to the next. Printed matter, such as newspapers, made it possible for information to be gathered in a central office and for news items to be written more accurately. In 1844 Samuel Morse perfected a system of sending coded messages through electrical wires, establishing an early form of long-distance communication. The network of communications expanded in 1858 through the work of Julius von Reuter, who extended the reach of newspapers by telegraphing news bulletins to different countries. With each of these developments, the public marveled at the ingenuity of the communications pioneers and asked, "What will they think of next?"

They thought of plenty! Alexander Graham Bell conceived of the idea of transmitting speech by electrical impulses and perfected the first telephone in 1876. The invention of the *wireless* by Guglielmo Marconi in 1895 paved the way for modern-day radio transmission. In 1928 V. K. Zworykin developed one of the first televisions.

Communications reached new heights when televisions were mass-produced in the 1950s. The 1962 launching of Telstar, the first communications satellite, enabled people to witness live events broadcast from anywhere in the world. Underground and underwater cables also began to transmit programs from one area to another, increasing the efficiency of information dissemination.

Nowadays, people can send messages anywhere in the world on their fax machines or through electronic mail on their computers in just a matter of seconds. Telecommunications and computer networking are testimonies to the enormous technological advances of our times and hint at even greater developments to come.

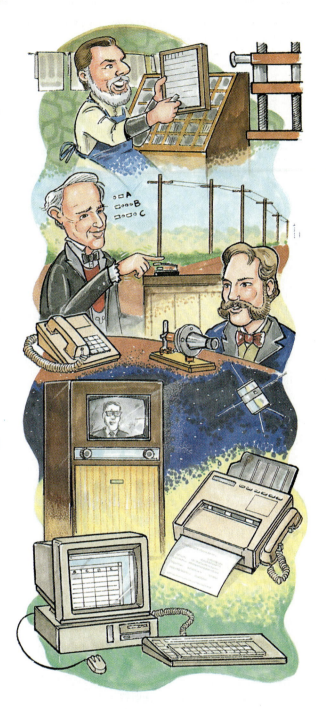

Interview several people, both students in your class and other people you know. Ask them the most important ways they receive information in their daily lives. Write down their answers.

Then discuss with the class: Which of these forms of communication existed 5 or 10 years ago? How about 50 years ago? Talk with the class about how communication has changed in our lifetimes.

A TV news reporter is interviewing someone who has just saved a little boy at the beach. Practice this interview with a partner.

A. What happened?
B. Well, I was lying on the beach listening to the radio, when suddenly I heard someone shouting for help.
A. So what did you do?
B. I jumped up, looked out toward the ocean, and saw a little boy waving his arms in the air.
A. **What did you do next?**[1]
B. I took off my shirt and my watch and jumped into the water.
A. **And THEN what did you do?**[1]
B. I swam out to the little boy, held him so his head stayed above water, and brought him back to shore.
A. That sounds like it was quite an experience!
B. It sure was!

A. What happened?
B. Well, I was _____ing, when suddenly _____.
A. So what did you do?
B. _____.
A. **What did you do next?**[1]
B. _____.
A. **And THEN what did you do?**[1]
B. _____.
A. That sounds like it was quite an experience!
B. It sure was!

---

[1] What did you do next?   What did you do after that?
     And then what did you do?   What was the next thing you did?

With your partner, create original scenes based on the situations below. You can use the model on page 46 as a guide, but feel free to adapt and expand it any way you wish.

1.

2.

3. Create your own series of events.

Function Review: *Chapters 1, 2, 3*

Choose the most appropriate line for Speaker B.

	A	**B**
1.	I'm going to Alaska.	a. How are you doing? b. What do you want to know? ⓒ That's fantastic!
2.	His company went out of business last year.	a. I'm absolutely positive. b. What a shame! c. How do you do?
3.	I'm going to a job interview, and I'm not sure what to wear.	a. I'm very sorry to hear that. b. Have you heard anything else? c. How about your blue suit?
4.	The weather is very pleasant in Georgia, and in my opinion, the people there are very nice.	a. What else can you tell me? b. How about you? c. How are things?
5.	Word has it that Larry has a new girlfriend.	a. I forgot all about it. b. I'm very happy for you. c. You're kidding!
6.	Tell me a little about yourself.	a. What else have you heard? b. What would you like to know? c. I'm absolutely positive!
7.	I haven't seen you in so long. How have you been?	a. I'm glad to meet you. b. Excuse me. c. Not bad.
8.	You didn't by any chance remember to turn on the dryer, did you?	a. I'm sure. b. Which one is that? c. Oh, it completely slipped my mind.
9.	Everybody says she's wonderful.	a. Really? That's interesting. b. What a pity! c. What do you do?
10.	Somehow I thought he was going to arrive later than you.	a. Okay. b. I don't think so. c. I forgot all about it.

Choose the most appropriate line for Speaker A.

	A	**B**
11.	a. Nice to meet you. b. I was going for a walk, when suddenly I heard a scream. c. I'm going to Florida next week.	So what did you do?
12.	a. How far did you travel? b. Did anybody call me? c. Do you know where the supermarket is?	Not as far as I know.
13.	a. How about you? b. Are you leaving soon? c. Did your mother have anything to say?	Not really. We just talked for a few minutes.
14.	a. I don't think we've met. b. How are you? c. Guess who I saw yesterday!	I'm Sam.

Choose the correct expression.

15. _____ by any chance know where the bus stop is?
a. Do you
b. Have you
c. Will you

16. Can you tell me _____?
a. what it's like
b. what did you do next more
c. where did you hear that

17. He's _____ with the blond hair.
a. the one
b. who
c. the boy who

18. _____ tell me anything else?
a. Will
b. Don't you
c. Can you

19. Let me _____ to my cousin, Jim.
a. meet you
b. tell you something more
c. introduce you

20. I'm very happy _____ that.
a. do you know
b. as far as I know
c. to hear

In Your Own Words

For Writing and Discussion

The people on pages 46 and 47 had some very scary experiences. Have YOU had any *traumatic experiences* in your life? Tell about one.

Here are the expressions you practiced in Chapter 3. Try to use as many as you can to expand your vocabulary and to add variety to your use of English.

Asking for and Reporting Information

Which one is that?

Have you by any chance ever _____ed?

Can you tell me what it's like?

Do you (by any chance) know _____?
Would you (by any chance) know _____?

Do you happen to know _____?
Would you happen to know _____?

Did you hear that _____?

What happened?

Where did you hear that?
How do you know (that)?
Who told you (that)?

I heard it on the radio/on TV/on the news.
I saw/read it in the paper.

School isn't really going to be closed tomorrow, is it?

Asking for and Reporting Additional Information

Can you tell me anything else?
Can you tell me anything more?
What else can you tell me?

What did you do next?
What did you do after that?
And then what did you do?
What was the next thing you did?

What else would you like to know?

As a matter of fact, . . .
In fact, . . .

Describing

It's the one with the _____.

It's a (very) _____.

It's one of the _____est _____s I know.

Identifying

The one *the children gave you.*

Certainty/Uncertainty

Inquiring about . . .

Are you positive/certain/sure (about that)?

Expressing Certainty

I'm positive/certain/sure.
I'm absolutely positive/certain/sure.
I'm a hundred percent sure.
There's no doubt about it.
I'm absolutely positive.

Expressing Uncertainty

I don't know for sure.
I'm not (completely) positive.
I'm not absolutely positive.
I'm not a hundred percent positive.

I don't think so.
Not as far as I know.

I doubt it.

Remembering/Forgetting

Inquiring about . . .

Don't you remember?
You remember.

Did you remember to _____?
Did you happen to remember to _____?
You didn't remember to _____, did you?
You didn't by any chance remember to _____, did you?

Indicating

I forgot (all about it).
I completely forgot.
It (completely) slipped my mind.

Oh, that one.

Surprise–Disbelief

School isn't really going to be closed tomorrow, is it?

They're going to make the park across the street into a parking lot?!

You're kidding!
No kidding!
You're joking!
I don't believe it!
I can't believe it!
Oh, come on!
No!
That can't be!
You've got to be kidding!

Focusing Attention

As a matter of fact, . . .
In fact, . . .

In my opinion, . . .
If you ask me, . . .
As far as I'm concerned, . . .

Initiating a Topic

Have you heard the news?

These scenes review the functions and conversation strategies in Chapters 1, 2, and 3. Who do you think these people are? What do you think they're talking about? With other students, improvise conversations based on these scenes and act them out.

1.

2.

3.

4.

5.

6.

7.

8.

4

REQUESTS
DIRECTIONS AND INSTRUCTIONS
CHECKING UNDERSTANDING
ASKING FOR REPETITION

Tim can't hear what his boss is asking him to do. What do you think Tim and his boss are saying to each other?

Minh is lost! A helpful person is giving her directions. What do you think they're saying to each other?

(1) I didn't hear you.
I didn't (quite) catch that.
I missed that.

(2) What did you say?
Could you (please) repeat that?
Would you (please) repeat that?
Could you say that again?
Would you say that again?
Would you mind saying that again?
Would you mind repeating that?

A. Would you mind playing your radio someplace else?
B. I'm sorry. **I didn't hear you.**(1) **What did you say?**(2)
A. I asked you if you'd play your radio someplace else.
B. Sure. I'd be happy to.
A. Thanks.

1.

2.

3.

4.

5.

Make a request.
Ask somebody to do
something.

Listening: *What's the Situation?*

Listen and choose the best answer.

1. a. He asked her to study with him.
   b. He asked her to turn on the radio.
   c. He couldn't study because her radio was disturbing him.

2. a. He offered to carry her bags.
   b. He didn't want to carry her bags.
   c. He told her to carry her bags.

3. a. He asked her to get thirty-two books.
   b. He asked her to repeat what she had read in the book.
   c. He told her what page to look at, but she didn't hear him.

4. a. She gave him a wrench.
   b. She was tired.
   c. She gave him her hand.

5. a. He asked her to turn off the stereo and go to sleep.
   b. He asked her to turn on the stereo.
   c. He asked her to turn down the stereo.

6. a. He tried to give her directions, but she didn't hear him.
   b. He was trying to catch a bus.
   c. He wanted to know if he was right.

7. a. She didn't hear him because she wasn't near him.
   b. She didn't hear him because she was copying the report.
   c. She didn't hear him ask her to copy the report.

InterAct!

"Noise Makers!"

In groups of four, think of a place and some noise that might be heard there. For example:

a factory
[noisy machinery]

someone's home
[children making noise]

a restaurant kitchen
[clattering dishes and shouted food orders]

a hair salon
[a fire alarm next door]

a hospital nursery
[babies crying]

a rock concert
[loud rock music]

Create a role play in which two of you are attempting to talk. The other two are making sounds that make it difficult for the two people speaking to hear each other. Present your *noise maker* role plays to the class.

(1) WHEN do you want me to
WHEN should I
WHEN did you tell me to

A. Please report for work tomorrow at 7:45.
B. I'm sorry. I didn't hear you. **WHEN do you want me to**(1) report for work tomorrow?
A. At 7:45.
B. Oh, okay.

Give somebody some instructions.

Grammar Check: *WH- Questions*

Choose the correct question word for Speaker B.

	A	**B**
1.	Please be here by 6:00 A.M.	(Where (When) How) do you want me to be here?
2.	Give these packages to the people in Apartment 2C.	(Who Where What) do you want me to give these to?
3.	Get two loaves of bread and some butter at the supermarket. Okay?	(Where What How) do you want me to get?
4.	Take these vitamins twice a day.	(What How often How) do you want me to take them?
5.	Put three coins in the machine.	(How much How How many) coins should I put in?
6.	I'm leaving for Mexico on the 9:00 A.M. flight.	(How often Where When) are you leaving for Mexico?
7.	Our English course ends very soon.	(When Which Why) course ends very soon?

"Fast Talker!"

The Characters: Choose a partner. One of you is a *boss* and the other is an *employee.* Decide on the place where you both work.

The Situation: The boss wants the employee to do several things and makes a list that includes what to do, when to do it, and where.

The Problem: The boss is a *fast talker*! When giving the employee directions, he or she speaks VERY quickly and energetically. As a result, the employee has a lot of trouble understanding everything the boss is saying.

Create a role play between the fast-talking boss and the employee and present it to the class.

Go to the corner and turn right.
Walk two blocks to Main Street.
Turn left, walk two more blocks, and you'll see the post office next to the bank.

get to the post office

A. **Could you please tell me**[1] how to get to the post office?
B. Sure. Go to the corner and turn right. Walk two blocks to Main Street. Turn left, walk two more blocks, and you'll see the post office next to the bank. **Have you got it?**[2]
A. I think so. **Let me see.**[3] First, I go to the corner and turn right.
B. **Uh-húh.**[4]
A. Then I walk two blocks to Main Street. Right?
B. **Um-hḿm.**[4]
A. And then I . . . Hmm. I forgot the last part. What do I do after that?
B. You turn left, walk two more blocks, and you'll see the post office next to the bank.
A. Okay.
B. Do you think you've got it now?
A. I think so. Thanks very much.

[1] Could you (please) tell me
Could you possibly tell me
Do you (by any chance) know
Would you (by any chance) know
Can you (please) tell me
Would you (possibly) be able to
    tell me
Would you by any chance be able
    to tell me
	[2] Have you got it?
	Got it?
	Have you got that?
	Got that?
	Do you follow me?
	Okay?
	
	[3] Let me see.
	Let me see if I understand.
	Let me see if I've got that.
	Let me see if I've got that right.
		[4] Uh-húh.
		Um-hḿm.
		Yes.
		That's right.
		Right.

A. **Could you please tell me**[1] how to _____?
B. Sure. _____.
_____.
_____.

Have you got it?[2]
A. I think so. **Let me see.**[3]
First, I _____.
B. **Uh-húh.**[4]
A. Then I _____. Right?
B. **Um-hḿm.**[4]
A. And then I . . . Hmm. I forgot the last part. What do I do after that?
B. You _____.
A. Okay.
B. Do you think you've got it now?
A. I think so. Thanks very much.

- *Pick up the receiver.*
- *Put in the money.*
- *Wait for the dial tone and dial.*

1. use this telephone

- *Pick up the nozzle.*
- *Put the nozzle in the gas tank.*
- *Press the handle to start the gas flowing.*

2. work the gas pump

- *Use the jack to raise up the car.*
- *Unscrew the bolts and take off the flat tire.*
- *Put on the new tire, put the bolts on tight, and lower the car.*

3. change a flat tire

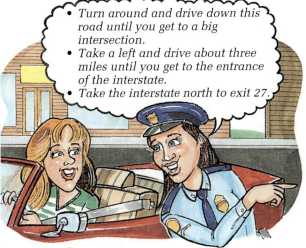

- *Turn around and drive down this road until you get to a big intersection.*
- *Take a left and drive about three miles until you get to the entrance of the interstate.*
- *Take the interstate north to exit 27.*

4. get to the airport

Give somebody some multi-step instructions and check to make sure the person understands.

Listening: *Getting Around Town*

Listen and follow the directions to different places on the map. Choose the letter that shows the place you're going to. The directions will always begin from *point X*.

1. a. A
   b. B
   c. C

2. a. D
   b. F
   c. M

3. a. R
   b. T
   c. P

4. a. G
   b. M
   c. L

5. a. O
   b. J
   c. K

6. a. P
   b. R
   c. Q

Vocabulary Check: *"Out of Place"*

Which word does not relate to the rest of the words in the group?

1. a. block   b. street   c. road   d. traffic
2. a. jack   b. lift   c. rest   d. raise
3. a. tight   b. secure   c. fixed   d. strong
4. a. fruit   b. nuts   c. bolts   d. screws
5. a. take away   b. take in   c. release   d. remove
6. a. unscrew   b. loosen   c. untwist   d. tighten
7. a. pump   b. explode   c. fill   d. inflate
8. a. tire   b. flat   c. deflated   d. empty
9. a. nozzle   b. spout   c. gas   d. faucet
10. a. tank   b. army   c. receptacle   d. compartment

There are many stereotypes about the character of people in various parts of the United States. In the Northeast and Midwest, people are said to be closed and private. In the South and West, they are often thought of as being more open and hospitable. Ask someone from St. Louis where the nearest sandwich shop is, and he or she will politely give you directions. A New Yorker might eye you suspiciously at first and, after deciding it is safe to talk to you, might give you a rather abrupt explanation. A person from Georgia might be very gracious about directing you and even suggest some alternative places to eat. A Texan just might take you to the place and treat you to lunch!

American stereotypes are abundant. New Englanders are often thought of as being friendly and helpful, but reserved. Southerners are known for their hospitality and warmth. People from the western part of the United States are often considered very outgoing. These variations in character can be traced to different factors such as climate, living conditions, and historical development.

When traveling from region to region, Americans themselves are often surprised at the differing degrees of friendliness in the United States.

InterCultural Connections

Is this also true for your country? Are people who live in different areas really different from each other?

There are many ways to describe people's characteristics and personalities. For example:

He's very closed.   *They're extremely polite.*   *She's a very warm person.*

Think of other words to describe people. Then tell which of these best describe the personalities and characteristics of people who live in different regions of your country.

What's your opinion? Do you think these are true characteristics, or are they stereotypes?

One friend is giving another a recipe for chocolate chip cookies. There are lots of instructions! Practice this scene with a partner.

A. Could you tell me your recipe for chocolate chip cookies?
B. Sure, but it's pretty complicated. You might want to write this down.
A. I'm afraid I don't have a pencil, but go ahead anyway.
B. Okay. First, mix together 2 cups of flour and a teaspoon of baking soda. Then add a teaspoon of salt. After that, mix together a cup of butter and a cup of sugar in a separate bowl. **Are you with me so far?**[1]
A. Yes. **I'm following you.**[2]
B. Okay. Then add 2 eggs. Next, combine all the ingredients in a large bowl. And then . . .
A. Wait a minute! **I didn't get that.**[3] Could you repeat the last two **instructions?**[4]
B. Sure. Add 2 eggs. And combine all the ingredients in a large bowl.
A. Okay. **I've got it.**[2]
B. Good. Now, where was I? Oh, yes. Slowly mix in a cup of chocolate chips and a cup of nuts. Then form little cookies from the mixture and place them on a cookie sheet. And finally, bake for 8 minutes at 375 degrees Fahrenheit. Have you got all that?
A. I think so. But let me repeat that back to make sure. First, I . . .

[1] Are you with me (so far)? Okay (so far)? Are you following me (so far)?	[2] I'm following you. I've got it. I understand. I see. I'm with you.	[3] I didn't get that. I'm lost. I'm not following you.	[4] instructions directions steps things you said

A. Could you tell me _____?
B. Sure, but it's pretty complicated. You might want to write this down.
A. I'm afraid I don't have a pencil, but go ahead anyway.
B. Okay. First, _____.
   Then _____.
   After that, _____.
   Are you with me so far?[1]
A. Yes. **I'm following you.**[2]
B. Okay. Then _____.
   Next, _____.
   And then . . .
A. Wait a minute! **I didn't get that.**[3] Could you repeat the last two **instructions**?[4]
B. Sure. _____.
   And _____.
A. Okay. **I've got it.**[2]
B. Good. Now, where was I? Oh, yes.
   _____.
   Then, _____.
   And finally, _____.
   Have you got all that?
A. I think so. But let me repeat that back to make sure. First, I . . .

Write out a list of 8 steps to do something (for example, directions to a place, how to make or repair something, or a recipe).

Now create an original scene with your partner, using the list of instructions. You can use the model above as a guide, but feel free to adapt and expand it any way you wish. Your partner should repeat back your instructions to make sure he or she understands you.

Function Check: *What's the Expression?*

A

B

1. _____ know how to get to the bank?
   a. Could you by any chance
   b. Would you be able
   c. Do you by any chance

2. Walk three blocks, turn left, and then go right. _____?
   a. Have you follow me?
   b. Let me understand?
   c. Okay?

3. _____.
   a. Okay?
   b. I'm with you.
   c. You follow me.

4. _____ where the post office is?
   a. Do you possible know
   b. Could you possibly tell me
   c. Would you chance know

5. _____.
   a. I've got it on the corner.
   b. Got it? It's on the corner.
   c. Sure. It's on the corner.

6. _____ show me how to use this pump?
   a. Would possible
   b. Do you know
   c. Could you

7. Pick up the nozzle, put it in the tank, and press the handle to start. _____?
   a. Now are you lost?
   b. Are you with me so far?
   c. Didn't you see?

8. I'm lost. _____ how to find School Street?
   a. Can you tell me
   b. Would you by any chance
   c. Can you please

9. Go down Rice Road and take the second left. _____?
   a. Did you have it?
   b. Have you get it?
   c. Have you got it?

10. Mix together four eggs, salt, pepper, and milk. _____?
    a. Now are you lost?
    b. Are you with me so far?
    c. Didn't you see?

11. Could you repeat _____?
    a. where are you
    b. the direction things you said
    c. the last two instructions

12. I'm not _____ you.
    a. lost
    b. following
    c. get

Listening: *The Best Response*

Listen and choose the best response.

1. a. Yes, that's right.
   b. Do you follow me?
   c. Sure. ⊛

2. a. I haven't.
   b. I think you understand.
   c. I think so.

3. a. I follow you.
   b. Uh-húh.
   c. Thank you.

4. a. Then what do I do?
   b. I forget.
   c. Do you follow me?

5. a. Let me understand.
   b. It's possibly.
   c. Sure.

6. a. Yes, it's far.
   b. Yes, I'm mixed up.
   c. Yes, I see.

7. a. No, I haven't.
   b. No. I'm afraid I didn't get that.
   c. No. I'm not understanding.

8. a. Yes. I'm lost.
   b. Okay. I've got it.
   c. No. I lost the instructions.

Listening: *What Process Is Being Described?*

Listen and decide what process is being described.

1. a. buying a can of soda
   b. making a deposit
   c. buying candy ⊛

2. a. taping together a piece of paper
   b. starting a tape recorder
   c. turning off a tape recorder

3. a. giving directions to a store
   b. writing a check
   c. making a calendar

4. a. locking up a car
   b. starting a fire
   c. starting a car with an alarm system

5. a. sewing a button
   b. taking a picture
   c. taking an eye exam

6. a. turning on a light
   b. making a lamp
   c. changing a light bulb

InterChange

Some people are *handy*. They know how to repair almost everything around the house! Some people have a *green thumb*. They seem to be able to make flowers and plants grow anywhere . . . both outdoors and indoors. Other people are *natural cooks*. They love to cook, and everything they make tastes out of this world!

Tell about the things you're good at. If you're *handy*, give some useful instructions for repairing something. If you have a *green thumb*, share some of your plant and flower secrets. And if you consider yourself a *natural cook*, share your favorite recipe.

Here are the expressions you practiced in Chapter 4. Try to use as many as you can to expand your vocabulary and to add variety to your use of English.

Asking for Repetition

I didn't hear you.
I didn't (quite) catch that.
I didn't get that.
I missed that.
I'm lost.
I'm not following you.

What did you say?
Could you (please) repeat that?
Would you (please) repeat that?
Could you say that again?
Would you say that again?
Would you mind saying that again?
Would you mind repeating that?

Could you repeat the last two
{ instructions?
  directions?
  steps?
  things you said?

WHEN do you want me to _____?
WHEN should I _____?
WHEN did you tell me to _____?

I forgot the last part.

Instructing

(Please) _____.

First, . . .
Then . . .
After that, . . .
Next, . . .
And finally, . . .

Directions–Location

Giving Directions

Go to _____.
Turn _____.
Walk _____ blocks.

Checking and Indicating Understanding

Checking Another Person's Understanding

Have you got it?
Got it?
Have you got that?
Got that?
Do you follow me?
Okay?

Are you with me (so far)?
Okay (so far)?
Are you following me (so far)?

Do you think you've got it now?
Have you got all that?

Checking One's Own Understanding

Let me see.
Let me see if I understand.
Let me see if I've got that.
Let me see if I've got that right.
Let me repeat that back.

Indicating Understanding

I'm following you.
I've got it.
I understand.
I see.
I'm with you.

Uh-húh.
Um-hḿm.
Yes.
That's right.
Right.

Asking for and Reporting Information

Could you (please) tell me _____?
Could you possibly tell me _____?
Do you (by any chance) know _____?
Would you (by any chance) know _____?
Can you (please) tell me _____?
Would you (possibly) be able to tell me _____?
Would you by any chance be able to tell me _____?

Requests

Direct, Polite

Please _____.

Direct, More Polite

Would you mind _____ing?

COMPLIMENTING
SATISFACTION AND
DISSATISFACTION
LIKES AND DISLIKES

Rosa is shopping for a dress for her senior prom. What do you think Rosa, her mother, and the salesperson are saying to each other?

Robert and Wanda didn't like the movie they just saw. What do you think they're saying to each other as they leave the theater?

performance

(1) a very good
    quite a

    [less formal]
    some

(2) Yes.
    Absolutely.

(3) excellent
    wonderful
    terrific
    magnificent
    fabulous
    superb

(4) Thanks (for saying so).
    Thank you (for saying so).
    It's nice of you to say so.
    It's nice of you to say that.

A. That was **a very good**[1] performance!
B. Did you really like it?
A. **Yes.**[2] I thought it was **excellent.**[3]
B. **Thanks for saying so.**[4]

1. dinner

2. lecture

3. presentation

4. party

5. speech

Compliment somebody.

(1) (really) like
love

(2) very
so

(3) Oh/Aw, go on!
Oh/Aw, come on!
Oh!

(4) I mean it!
I'm (really) serious.
I'm being honest with you.

apartment
spacious

A. I **really like**(1) your apartment. It's **very**(2) spacious.
B. **Oh, go on!**(3) You're just saying that!
A. No. **I mean it!**(4) It's one of the most spacious apartments I've ever seen.
B.. Well, thanks for saying so. I'm glad you like it.

1. tie
attractive

2. dress
pretty

3. painting
interesting

4. blouse
colorful

5. haircut
nice

Be modest when somebody compliments you.

Function Check: *What's My Line?*

Choose the most appropriate line for Speaker B.

	A		**B**
1.	I really like your necklace. It's very attractive!	a. b. c.	I'm not really serious. I'm being nice to you. Oh, go on! (c circled)
2.	That suit is one of the nicest suits I've ever seen!	a. b. c.	Thanks for being honest. Oh, come on! You're just saying that! I'm really honest.
3.	Your new hairstyle is really wonderful!	a. b. c.	Absolutely. Fabulous. Thanks.
4.	Oh, go on! You're just saying that!	a. b. c.	Well, I'm glad. No, thanks. No. I mean it.
5.	You've written the most interesting and unusual poems!	a. b. c.	Well, it's nice. Well, thanks for saying so. Well, I'm glad you're going on.
6.	I really love your glasses. They're so stylish!	a. b. c.	I've never seen them. I'm glad you like them. It's nice of you for saying so.

Listening: *Where Are They?*

Listen and decide where each conversation is taking place.

1. a. at a play (circled)
   b. at a gas station
   c. at a playground

2. a. in a supermarket
   b. at a restaurant
   c. at a bakery

3. a. in a fresh-vegetable store
   b. at a photography exhibit
   c. at a university

4. a. in a drug store
   b. in a department store
   c. at an advertising agency

5. a. in an office
   b. in a library
   c. at a tennis court

6. a. at someone's home
   b. at City Hall
   c. at a movie theater

7. a. in a music store
   b. at the symphony
   c. at a pastry shop

8. a. on a farm
   b. in a supermarket
   c. at a school

9. a. in a camera store
   b. in an art class
   c. at a bank

Listen and decide what the relationship between the two speakers is.

1. a. teacher–parent
   b. brother–sister
   c. actor–director

2. a. banker–customer
   b. doctor–patient
   c. accountant–client

3. a. mechanic–customer
   b. husband–wife
   c. teacher–student

4. a. professor–student
   b. employer–employee
   c. employee–employer

5. a. ticket taker–moviegoer
   b. librarian–student
   c. police officer–driver

6. a. father–child
   b. customer-waiter
   c. pianist–audience member

7. a. student–student
   b. lawyer–criminal
   c. nurse–doctor

8. a. mother–child
   b. homeowner–gardener
   c. customer–laundry owner

9. a. real estate agent–client
   b. politician–supporter
   c. shop owner–customer

Reading: *Accepting Compliments*

Everyone needs a *pat on the back* now and then, but compliments are often easier to give than to receive, especially for Americans. Tell an American that he or she plays a great game of tennis, and the compliment will probably be shrugged off with "It must be my lucky day" or "This new racket is wonderful" or "My tennis teacher is fantastic!" Of course, a person might also smile and say "Thank you," but many Americans downplay compliments by giving the credit to someone or something else.

It is interesting to compare how people from different cultures react to compliments. In some countries, if you compliment someone on a possession, he or she will give it to you or tell you that you may use it whenever you like. In some countries, a person will make a derogatory remark about it or show humility and unworthiness of praise. But in most cultures, compliments are received with gratitude.

A current form of complimenting is referred to as *stroking*, the praise or positive feedback people give each other, especially at the workplace. American companies understand the importance of giving recognition to employees in order to maintain morale and assure worker performance. Companies often give rewards for outstanding achievement and service.

InterCultural Connections

In your country, do people often compliment others? What do they compliment them about? What are the most common ways of complimenting others? And how do people usually react when they receive compliments?

bicycle
heavy
large

(1) How do you like
What do you think of

(2) fine
very nice
perfect

(3) satisfied
happy
pleased

(4) Very.
Very much.
Yes.

(5) just what I had in mind/
wanted/was looking
for

A. **How do you like**[1] the bicycle?
B. It's **fine**.[2]
A. It isn't too heavy?
B. No, not at all.
A. Is it large enough?
B. Oh, yes. I wouldn't want it any larger.
A. So you're **satisfied**[3] with it?
B. **Very**.[4] It's **just what I had in mind!**[5]

1. mattress
short
firm

2. tennis racket
big
light

3. wedding dress
plain
fancy

4. gloves
bulky
warm

5. pants
tight
long

Express your
satisfaction about
something.

Grammar Check: *TOO and ENOUGH*

1. Ted is six feet three inches tall. There's a bed he wants to buy, but it's only six feet long.
   a. The bed is too long.
   ⓑ The bed isn't long enough.

2. Sara has a twenty-eight inch waist. There's a skirt she wants to buy, but it only has a twenty-four-inch waist.
   a. The skirt is too tight.
   b. The skirt isn't tight enough.

3. Ed is going to a formal party, and he needs to buy a new suit to wear.
   a. His old suit is too formal.
   b. His old suit isn't formal enough.

4. Diane wears size six shoes. However, she has found a pair of size eight shoes she likes very much.
   a. The shoes are too big.
   b. The shoes aren't big enough.

5. Marcia needs a new mattress because she has a bad back. Her friend offered her a mattress, but it didn't help at all.
   a. The mattress was soft enough.
   b. The mattress was too soft.

6. Jennifer needs to wrap a large gift, but she only has a very small box.
   a. The box isn't too large.
   b. The box isn't large enough.

7. Jane wants to wear her new winter coat outside, but it's seventy degrees.
   a. The coat is warm enough.
   b. The coat is too warm.

8. The teacher wanted to challenge her students, but she gave them a very easy assignment.
   a. The assignment was easy enough.
   b. The assignment was too easy.

Listening: *What's the Customer Buying?*

Listen and decide what each customer is buying.

1. ⓐ a mattress
   b. a dress
   c. a typewriter

2. a. a blouse
   b. a book
   c. a tennis racket

3. a. a ring
   b. a coat
   c. a chair

4. a. shoes
   b. umbrellas
   c. socks

5. a. a sweater
   b. fruit
   c. a stereo

6. a. a radio
   b. a dress
   c. a pair of glasses

InterChange

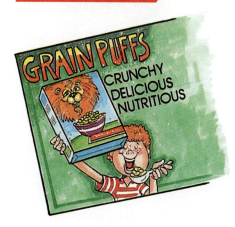

Be creative! Design an advertisement for a product!

Decide on the product, give it a name, and think of some key words to describe that product. (For example, a cereal might be described as *crunchy*, *delicious*, and *nutritious*.)

Present your advertisements to the class and have students vote on the most creative and convincing ad!

hat
old-fashioned
stylish

(1) What seems to be the problem (with it)?
What seems to be the matter (with it)?
What's the problem (with it)?
What's the matter (with it)?
What's wrong (with it)?

(2) I don't think so.
Not really.
Probably not.

(3) However,
But

A. I'd like to return this hat.
B. **What seems to be the problem with it?**(1)
A. It's too old-fashioned.
B. Would you like to exchange it for one that's more stylish?
A. **I don't think so.**(2) I'd just like a refund, please.
B. I'm sorry. We don't give refunds. **However,**(3) we'll be happy to offer you credit toward another purchase in our store.
A. No refunds?
B. I'm afraid not.
A. Oh. Thanks anyway.

1. coat
long
short

2. sport shirt
flashy
conservative

3. home repair book
complicated
simple

4. video game
easy
challenging

5. parrot
talkative
quiet

Express dissatisfaction with something and return it where you bought it.

Grammar Check: *Adjectives*

1. Anne's directions were confusing. Bob's were _____ than hers.
   a. too simple
   b. any simpler
   c. much simpler *(circled)*

2. Everybody looks up to Linda because she's _____ student in our class.
   a. smart enough
   b. the smarter
   c. the smartest

3. Those children never stop talking! They're certainly _____ than any other children I know!
   a. the most talkative
   b. more talkative
   c. any more talkative

4. Ken has several tennis rackets. His ten-year-old son wants to borrow one, but they're all _____ for his small hand.
   a. too big
   b. big enough
   c. bigger

5. My mother and father never agree about politics. My father is _____ my mother.
   a. too conservative as
   b. more conservative than
   c. as conservative as

6. Roger doesn't like to study very much. His older brother studies all the time. Roger isn't _____ his older brother.
   a. the most serious
   b. as serious as
   c. serious enough

7. Brenda's sports car is bright red like a fire engine! Everybody on our street says it's _____ car they've ever seen.
   a. flashier
   b. flashy
   c. the flashiest

8. Timmy is only five feet tall. The rest of the people in his family are very tall. No one is _____ he is.
   a. short enough as
   b. shorter than
   c. the shortest as

InterChange

Have you ever tried to return anything to a store?

Why did you want to return it?
Did the store take the item back, or did they refuse?

Tell about your experience.

the play
funny

(1) to tell (you) the truth,
honestly,
to be honest (with you),

(2) I was (a little) disappointed.
I wasn't very pleased with it.
It was (a little) disappointing.

(3) Why?
How come?

(4) expected it to be
thought it would be
hoped it would be

A. How did you like the play?
B. Well, **to tell the truth,**(1) **I was a little disappointed.**(2)
A. **Why?**(3)
B. It wasn't as funny as I thought it would be.
   I really **expected it to be**(4) a lot funnier.
A. That's too bad.

1. your vacation
   relaxing

2. the game
   exciting

3. the steak
   juicy

4. your date with Ted last night
   enjoyable

5. English class today
   good

Tell somebody why you were disappointed about something.

Listening: *What's the Meaning?*

Listen and choose the answer that is closest in meaning to the sentence you have heard.

1. a. I didn't think the movie would be good.
    b. I didn't like the movie very much. *(circled)*
    c. The movie will be good.

2. a. You didn't tell me the truth about my grades.
    b. You were disappointed with my grades.
    c. My grades were disappointing.

3. a. I hoped the class wouldn't be any shorter.
    b. I hoped the class would be shorter.
    c. I hoped for a long class.

4. a. I didn't think Howard was honest with you.
    b. Howard couldn't have been nicer.
    c. Howard was nice.

5. a. Were you disappointed you came?
    b. Why were you pleased?
    c. Why were you disappointed?

6. a. Brian was dishonest.
    b. The company was not pleased with Brian's work.
    c. Brian was disappointed with the work the company did for him.

7. a. I thought Linda's presentation would be uninteresting.
    b. I didn't think about Linda's presentation.
    c. Linda was interested in my thoughts about her presentation.

8. a. John's partner was challenged.
    b. John was challenged.
    c. John didn't expect his partner to be bad.

9. a. Honestly, it was terrible.
    b. You were terribly honest.
    c. I thought you were honest.

10. a. The score of the game was disappointing.
    b. The baseball player wasn't playing in the game.
    c. The game wasn't being scored.

11. a. I expected the waterfalls to be spectacular.
    b. The waterfalls were wonderful.
    c. I expected the waterfalls to be boring.

InterChange

Disappointments

Unfortunately, we've all had times in our lives when things didn't turn out as well as we would have liked.

Talk with a partner about disappointments you've had, and then share your stories with the class.

My landlord is always forgetting to fix things.

(1) annoyed with
upset with

[stronger]
mad at
angry at
furious with

(2) *He's* always
He's constantly
He keeps on

(3) bothers
annoys
upsets

(4) mention it to *him*
talk to *him* about it
discuss it with *him*
bring up the subject
with *him*

A. I'm really **annoyed with**[1] my landlord.
B. Why?
A. **He's always**[2] forgetting to fix things.
B. Have you spoken to him about it?
A. Well, actually not.
B. I don't understand. If it **bothers**[3] you so much, why don't you **mention it to him**?[4]
A. I guess I should. But I don't like to complain.

1. My secretary is always making spelling mistakes.

2. My neighbors are always playing their stereo past midnight.

3. My teacher is always giving us homework over the weekend.

4. My roommate is always snoring at night.

5. My parents are always treating me like a baby.

Tell a friend about somebody you're annoyed with.

Grammar Check: *Tense Review*

A **B**

1. _____ to your boss about changing your work hours?
   a. Has you spoken
   b. Have you speak
   ⓒ Have you spoken

2. No. I _____ mentioned it to her yet.
   a. don't
   b. haven't
   c. do

3. My neighbors are always _____ me!
   a. upset with
   b. upsetting with
   c. upset

4. I _____ understand why you say that.
   a. haven't
   b. have
   c. don't

5. They tell me I constantly _____ my stereo late at night.
   a. playing
   b. to play
   c. play

6. _____ talk to them about it?
   a. Why don't
   b. Why don't you
   c. Why you

7. I guess I _____.
   a. did
   b. don't
   c. will

8. You really _____.
   a. ought
   b. ought of
   c. ought to

9. Why are you always _____ to feed your fish?
   a. forget
   b. forgot
   c. forgetting

10. I don't know why. I keep on _____ to do it!
    a. forget
    b. forgetting
    c. to forget

Talk to Them!

You've decided to talk to the people in situations 1–5 on the previous page about the things that are bothering you.

your secretary

your neighbors

your teacher

your roommate

your parents

With a partner, create conversations in which you try to solve these problems. Present your conversations to the class.

Two friends are trying to decide what to do this weekend. Practice this scene with a partner.

A. Would you like to get together this weekend?

B. Sure. What would you like to do?

A. Well, how about seeing a movie?

B. That sounds good. Did you have any particular movie in mind?

A. Well, they say that *A Man and His Horse* is very good. It's playing at the Rialto Theater.

B. *A Man and His Horse?* That's a **western**,[1] isn't it?

A. I think so.

B. Well, to tell the truth, **I don't like westerns**[1] **very much**.[2]

A. Oh. Well, is there any particular movie you'd like to see?

B. How about *The Return of the Monster?* It's playing at the Shopping Mall Cinema, and I hear it's excellent.

A. *The Return of the Monster?* Hmm. Isn't that a **science fiction movie?**[1]

B. Yes. Don't you like **science fiction movies**?[1]

A. No, not really. Maybe we shouldn't see a movie. Maybe we should do something else.

B. Okay. Would you be interested in doing something outdoors?

A. Sure. Any suggestions?

B. Well, we could go ice skating.

A. I'm afraid **I don't really enjoy**[2] going ice skating. How about going hiking?

B. Well, to tell the truth, I've gone hiking several times in the past few weeks.

A. Really? Then I guess you must be pretty **tired of**[3] hiking.

B. I am. Let's do something else.

A. Why don't we just have dinner together somewhere this Saturday?

B. That sounds like a good idea. Where would you like to go?

A. Well, one of my favorite places to eat is The Captain's Table.

B. The Captain's Table? What kind of food do they serve there?

A. **Seafood.**[4] But if you don't like **seafood,**[4] we can go someplace else.

B. No. On the contrary, I LOVE **seafood**![4]

A. You do?! Great!

B. Then **it's settled**.[5] The Captain's Table for dinner on Saturday. What time?

A. How about 7 o'clock?

B. Is 8 okay?

A. Fine.

A. Would you like to get together this weekend?
B. Sure. What would you like to do?
A. Well, how about seeing a movie?
B. That sounds good. Did you have any particular movie in mind?
A. Well, they say that _____ is very good. It's playing at the _____.
B. _____? That's a _____,(1) isn't it?
A. I think so.
B. Well, to tell the truth, **I don't like** _____s(1) **very much.**(2)
A. Oh. Well, is there any particular movie you'd like to see?
B. How about _____? It's playing at the _____, and I hear it's excellent.
A. _____? Hmm. Isn't that a _____?(1)
B. Yes. Don't you like _____s?(1)
A. No, not really. Maybe we shouldn't see a movie. Maybe we should do something else.
B. Okay. Would you be interested in doing something outdoors?
A. Sure. Any suggestions?
B. Well, we could go _____ing.
A. I'm afraid **I don't really enjoy**(2) going _____ing. How about going _____ing?
B. Well, to tell the truth, I've gone _____ing several times in the past few weeks.
A. Really? Then I guess you must be pretty **tired of**(3) _____ing.
B. I am. Let's do something else.
A. Why don't we just have dinner together somewhere this Saturday?
B. That sounds like a good idea. Where would you like to go?
A. Well, one of my favorite places to eat is _____.
B. _____? What kind of food do they serve there?
A. _____.(4) But if you don't like _____,(4) we can go someplace else.
B. No. On the contrary, I LOVE _____!(4)
A. You do?! Great!
B. Then **it's settled.**(5) _____ for dinner on Saturday. What time?
A. How about _____ o'clock?
B. Is _____ okay?
A. Fine.

Now create an original scene with your partner. Use the names of movies, theaters, and restaurants where you live, and refer to outdoor activities you enjoy doing on the weekend. You can use the model above as a guide, but feel free to adapt and expand it any way you wish.

Listening: *How Do They Feel?*

Listen and decide how Speaker B feels about Speaker A's suggestion.

1. a. likes the idea
   b. dislikes the idea *(circled)*

2. a. likes the idea
   b. dislikes the idea

3. a. likes the idea
   b. dislikes the idea

4. a. likes the idea
   b. dislikes the idea

5. a. likes the idea
   b. dislikes the idea

6. a. likes the idea
   b. dislikes the idea

7. a. likes the idea
   b. dislikes the idea

8. a. likes the idea
   b. dislikes the idea

9. a. likes the idea
   b. dislikes the idea

InterView

Favorite Restaurants

Take a survey of students in the class. Ask each person:

What's your favorite kind of food?
What's your favorite restaurant?

Report the results back to the class and compile a list of everybody's favorite foods and restaurants.

Favorite Recreational Activities

Ask students in the class about their favorite outdoor activities.

What outdoor activities do you enjoy?
How often do you do them?

Tell the class about your interviews and see which activities are the most popular.

Going to the Movies

There are many different kinds of movies:

dramas

comedies

mysteries

adventure movies

science fiction movies

documentaries

westerns

foreign films

children's films

cartoons

Talk with a partner about going to the movies.

What kind of movies do you like? Why?
What kind of movies don't you like? Why not?
How often do you go to the movies?
What are your "Top 10" favorite movies?

Tell the class about your conversations and make a list of everybody's movie favorites.

Be a Critic!

Write a newspaper review of a movie you recently saw. Tell about the acting, the directing, the photography, and the plot.

Did you like the movie? Tell why with appropriate *complimentary* expressions.

Did you dislike the movie? Tell why with appropriate expressions for *dislike* and *disappointment*.

Distribute everybody's reviews to the class.

Here are the expressions you practiced in Chapter 5. Try to use as many as you can to expand your vocabulary and to add variety to your use of English.

Satisfaction/Dissatisfaction

Inquiring about . . .

How do you like _____?
What do you think of _____?

How did you like _____?

Did you (really) like it?

Are you $\begin{cases} \text{satisfied} \\ \text{happy} \\ \text{pleased} \end{cases}$ with it?

Is it _____ enough?

What seems to be the problem (with it)?
What seems to be the matter (with it)?
What's the problem (with it)?
What's the matter (with it)?
What's wrong (with it)?

Expressing Satisfaction

It's $\begin{cases} \text{fine.} \\ \text{very nice.} \\ \text{perfect.} \end{cases}$

It's just what I $\begin{cases} \text{had in mind.} \\ \text{wanted.} \\ \text{was looking for.} \end{cases}$

I wouldn't want it any _____er.

Expressing Dissatisfaction

It's too _____.

I really $\begin{cases} \text{expected it to be} \\ \text{thought it would be} \\ \text{hoped it would be} \end{cases}$ _____er.

It wasn't as _____ as I thought it would be.

Gratitude

Expressing . . .

Thanks/Thank you (for saying so).
It's nice of you to say so/that.

Persuading–Insisting

I mean it!
I'm (really) serious.
I'm being honest with you.

Likes/Dislikes

Inquiring about . . .

How do you like _____?
What do you think of _____?
How did you like _____?
Did you like _____?
Don't you like _____?

Expressing Likes

I like _____.
I love _____.

Expressing Dislikes

I don't like _____ very much.
I don't enjoy _____ very much.
I don't (particularly) care for _____.
I'm not (really) crazy about _____.
[stronger]
I hate _____.

Complimenting

Expressing Compliments

That was $\begin{cases} \text{a very good} \\ \text{quite a} \\ \text{[less formal]} \\ \text{some} \end{cases}$ _____!

I thought it was $\begin{cases} \text{excellent.} \\ \text{wonderful.} \\ \text{terrific.} \\ \text{magnificent.} \\ \text{fabulous.} \\ \text{superb.} \end{cases}$

I (really) like _____.
I love _____.

It's very _____.
It's so _____.

It's one of the _____est _____s I've ever _____ed.

Responding to Compliments

Thanks (for saying so).
Thank you (for saying so).
It's nice of you to say so.
It's nice of you to say that.
I'm glad you like it.

Oh/Aw, go on!
Oh/Aw, come on!
Oh!

You're just saying that.

Disappointment

I was (a little) disappointed.
I wasn't very pleased with it.
It was (a little) disappointing.

Complaining

It's too _____.

I was (a little) disappointed.
I wasn't very pleased with it.
It was (a little) disappointing.

I'm $\begin{cases} \text{annoyed with} \\ \text{upset with} \\ \text{[stronger]} \\ \text{mad at} \\ \text{angry at} \\ \text{furious with} \end{cases}$ _____.

He's always
He's constantly $\Big\}$ _____ing.
He keeps on

It $\begin{cases} \text{bothers} \\ \text{annoys} \\ \text{upsets} \end{cases}$ me.

I'm tired of _____(ing).
I'm sick of _____(ing).
I'm sick and tired of _____(ing).

Advice–Suggestions

Asking for . . .

Any suggestions?

Offering . . .

How about _____?
How about _____ing?
Would you be interested in _____?
We could _____.
Why don't we _____?
Let's _____.

Why don't you _____?

Have you _____ed?

Maybe we should _____.
Maybe we shouldn't _____.

They say that _____ is very good.
One of my favorite _____s is _____.

Is _____ okay?

6

PREFERENCES
WANTS AND DESIRES

Mr. and Mrs. Salinas are ordering their meal, and their waitress is taking their order. What do you think they're saying to each other?

Howard wants to watch a certain TV show. Helen doesn't care what they watch. What do you think they're saying to each other?

I'd Prefer a Baked Potato

a steak
rare
a baked potato
a cup of coffee

a baked potato or rice?

(1) I'd like
     I'll have
     I want

(2) prefer
     rather have
     like

A. May I help you?
B. Yes, **I'd like**(1) a steak.
A. How would you like it?
B. Rare.
A. Okay. And would you **prefer**(2) a baked potato or rice with that?
B. I'd **prefer**(2) a baked potato.
A. Anything to drink?
B. A cup of coffee, please.
A. Okay. That's a rare steak with a baked potato and a cup of coffee.

a hamburger
well-done
french fries
a Coke

1. french fries or potato chips?

the chicken
baked
a salad
a glass of mineral water

2. a salad or a vegetable?

an order of eggs
scrambled
toast
a glass of milk

3. toast or a muffin?

a cheese sandwich
grilled
potato salad
a glass of lemonade

4. potato salad or cole slaw?

the fish
fried
noodles
a diet soda

5. mashed potatoes or noodles?

Order a complete meal in a restaurant.

Grammar Check: *Partitives*

1. I'd like _____ coffee, please.
   a. a bowl of
   b. a pound of *(circled)*
   c. a glass of

2. How about _____ rye bread for your ham and cheese sandwich?
   a. a few loaves of
   b. a few pounds of
   c. a few slices of

3. I'd like to have _____ spaghetti and meatballs, please.
   a. a box of
   b. a package of
   c. an order of

4. Could I have _____ milk to drink with this cookie, please?
   a. a glass of
   b. a quart of
   c. a gallon of

5. Mr. Cleary decided to cook a special meal, and so he bought _____ chicken for his family's dinner.
   a. a piece of
   b. a package of
   c. a leg of

6. The recipe called for _____ butter.
   a. a bowl of
   b. a pound of
   c. a bottle of

7. The chef used _____ lettuce to make a salad for five people.
   a. a piece of
   b. a head of
   c. a slice of

8. Let's get _____ strawberry jelly to go with these two muffins.
   a. a case of
   b. a jar of
   c. a bottle of

9.

I'm not very hungry. I'll just have _____ french fries with my hamburger.
   a. a pound of
   b. a few of
   c. a small dish of

I Changed My Mind!

The customers in the restaurants on page 86 have changed their minds!

I changed my mind. I'd rather have . . .

I think I'd prefer . . .

I'd like . . . instead of . . .

Choose one of the restaurant scenes on page 86. With a partner, create a role play between the customer and waiter or waitress. Present your role plays to the class.

I'd Much Rather See a Movie

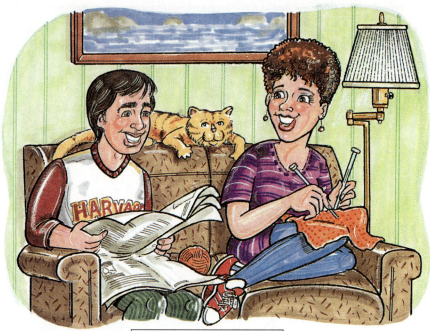

(1) Would you like to
Would you prefer to
Would you rather
Do you want to

(2) I'd prefer to
I'd rather
I'd like to

(3) I (really) don't feel like
_____ing.
I'm not (really) in the
mood to _____.
I'd (really) prefer not to
_____.

stay home or see a movie?

A. **Would you like to**(1) stay home or see a movie?
B. I think **I'd prefer to**(2) stay home. How about you?
A. Well, to be honest, **I really don't feel like** staying home.(3)
I'd much rather see a movie. Is that okay with you?
B. Sure. We haven't seen a movie in a long time.

1. eat at home or at a restaurant?

2. swim at the beach or in the pool?

3. walk home or take a taxi?

4. watch the game on TV or go to the stadium?

5. put Rover in the kennel or take him on vacation with us?

IMPORTANT MESSAGE
TO
WHILE YOU WERE OUT

Talk with somebody about what you'd prefer to do.

88

Function Check: *What's the Expression?*

	A	B
1.	Would you like to go swimming or play tennis?	Oh, I think I'd _____ to play tennis. a. rather (b.) like c. rather have
2.	How would you like your meat cooked?	I'd _____ it rare, please. a. rather b. like c. have
3.	Would you like to go skating today?	Well, I'm _____ to go out today. a. prefer not b. not feeling like c. not really in the mood
4.	_____ to go to the ballet with me next Saturday? a. Do you want b. Would you rather c. Would you prefer	Thanks very much, but I'm busy all next week.
5.	_____ leave right now? a. Do you like to b. Would you rather c. Would you	No. I don't mind staying a little longer.
6.	_____ to study alone. a. I'd prefer not to b. I'm not really in the mood c. I'd prefer	Okay. I'll leave you alone.

InterView

Take a poll of people in your class. Ask their opinion of the following:

> *What would you rather do this weekend: study English or . . . ?*

(Fill in any activity you wish.)

Report your findings back to the class and tabulate the results.

A. **You've seemed troubled**[1] for the past few days. Is anything **wrong**?[2]
B. Well, to tell the truth, I've been having a disagreement with my boss.
A. Oh? What's it all about?
B. Well, to make a long story short, my boss wants me to switch to the night shift, but I'd rather stay on the day shift.
A. Does he feel strongly about your switching to the night shift?
B. Yes, he does. And I feel just as strongly about staying on the day shift.
A. Well, it sounds like a serious disagreement. I hope you can **resolve it**[3] soon.
B. So do I.

[1] You've seemed troubled	[2] wrong	[3] resolve it
You've seemed upset	the matter	settle it
You've seemed preoccupied	going on	work it out
You haven't been yourself		

1. my mother

2. my wife

3. my parents

4. my business partner

5. my family

6. my husband

7. the people in my parish

8. my economic advisor

9. some members of my labor union

Grammar Check: WANT and WANT + Object + Infinitive

1. My husband _____ to move, but I want to stay here.
   a. wants them
   b. wants ⓑ
   c. prefers us

2. The president _____ Congress to raise taxes.
   a. prefers to
   b. wants
   c. would rather

3. The negotiators _____ more time to work out a compromise.
   a. want
   b. would rather
   c. want it

4. The car dealer _____ to make up my mind by the end of the week.
   a. wants me
   b. wants
   c. prefers

5. His wife _____ to open up a savings account.
   a. prefers him
   b. rather he
   c. wants him

6. His parents _____ to study more, but he prefers to go to parties.
   a. want
   b. want him
   c. want them

7. Dr. Peters _____ to have another operation, but Mrs. Clark didn't want her husband to have any more surgery.
   a. wanted him
   b. wanted
   c. wanted her

8. The manager _____ to give a report of your findings.
   a. would rather
   b. will want you
   c. will want it

9. The customers _____ to expand, but the owner doesn't want to.
   a. want the restaurant
   b. want
   c. prefer

10. *I wonder why the Internal Revenue Service _____ give them more copies of last year's tax return!*
    a. *would rather*
    b. *wants me to*
    c. *prefers I*

For Writing and Discussion

There are always *demands* in life—things other people want us to do.

My boss wants me to work overtime every day next week.

My wife wants me to help more around the house.

My father wants me to get better grades in school.

Tell about demands in YOUR life and how you feel about them.

Choose one of the conflicts presented on pages 90 and 91. With a partner, create a dramatization of the conflict. Which one will you choose to reenact?

the boss and employee

the mother and son

the wife and husband

the parents and daughter

the two business partners

the parents and children

the husband and wife

the priest and the people in his parish

the president and his economic advisor

the labor union members

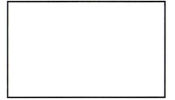

(the characters you created)

Present your drama to the class and ask people to suggest ways of resolving the conflict. After listening to others' advice, decide on the best way to resolve the conflict and act out your *conclusion* for the class.

InterChange

What's Your Opinion?

Talk with a partner about the following:

The employee on page 90 says he's having a disagreement with his boss. Do you think it's ever appropriate for an employee to argue with his or her boss? In what situations?

In one of the conflicts on page 91, a husband and wife are discussing putting her mother in a home for senior citizens. What's your opinion of this? Do you think this is a good idea? What typically happens in your country when an elderly person is no longer capable of living alone?

(1) have any strong feelings about it
have any feelings about it one way or another
care one way or the other
have a preference

(2) It doesn't make any difference (to me).
It doesn't matter (to me).
It's all the same to me.
I don't care.
I don't feel strongly about it one way or the other.

A. When do you want to leave?
B. Oh, I don't know. Whenever you'd like to leave is fine with me.
A. You don't **have any strong feelings about it**?(1)
B. No, not really. **It doesn't make any difference.**(2)

1.

2.

3.

4.

5.

Express indifference when somebody asks you something.

Grammar Check: *WH-ever Words*

Choose the best word to complete the sentence.

a. whatever	c. whoever	e. whichever
b. whenever	d. however	f. wherever

b 1. A. What time do you want to go home?
   B. _____ you want to leave is okay with me.

___ 2. A. What should I do with the car?
   B. You should park it _____ you find a space.

___ 3. A. I don't know whether to drive to the airport or take a taxi.
   B. _____ you get there, just make sure you aren't late for the plane!

___ 4. A. Who does she want me to tell?
   B. She wants you to tell her secretary _____ you can.

___ 5. A. Who makes the decisions about investments for the company?
   B. The president does _____ she thinks is best.

___ 6. A. I can't decide whether to buy the striped tie or the plaid one.
   B. Well, _____ one you buy will look great with that suit!

Listening: *Where Are They?*

Listen and decide where each conversation is taking place.

1. a. at a restaurant
   b. in a classroom
   c. at someone's home

2. a. at someone's home
   b. at a Chinese restaurant
   c. at an Italian restaurant

3. a. at a pet store
   b. at a florist
   c. at someone's home

4. a. in the dining room
   b. in the study
   c. in the bathroom

5. a. at someone's home
   b. at a bakery
   c. at a restaurant

6. a. at a political meeting
   b. at a gas station
   c. at someone's home

7. a. in a taxi cab
   b. in an office
   c. at a tennis court

8. a. in a paint store
   b. at someone's home
   c. in a boat

9. a. at a diner
   b. in someone's kitchen
   c. at a lake

InterView

Make a list of three important issues you feel strongly about. These might be topical issues that are currently being talked about in newspapers or on television, or perhaps they are more personal issues that you care a great deal about.

Interview other students in the class and find out how THEY feel about these issues. Do they feel the same way . . . or are they *indifferent*? Write down people's views and report back to the class.

go home early?

(1) Would you mind
Would it bother you
Would it disturb you

(2) It's (entirely) up to you.
It's (entirely) your
      decision.
It's for you to decide.

A. **Would you mind**(1) if I went home early?
B. No. I wouldn't mind.
A. Are you sure? I mean if you'd rather I didn't, I won't.
B. No. Honestly. It doesn't matter to me whether you go home early or not. **It's entirely up to you.**(2)

1. watch the news?

2. invite my boss for dinner?

3. drop something off at the post office?

4. go on a date with someone else?

5. take away your "security blanket"?

Express indifference when somebody makes a request.

Function Check: *What's My Line?*

Choose the appropriate line for Speaker B.

	A	B
1.	Would you mind if I took you home early?	a. It isn't up to you. (b.) It doesn't make any difference to me. c. It's for me to feel strongly about.
2.	Would you like to go swimming today?	a. It's entirely your matter. b. I wouldn't matter. c. I don't care. It's for you to decide.
3.	Would it disturb you if I turned on the baseball game?	a. No, I wouldn't mind. b. No, it's entirely your preference. c. No, it's all the same.
4.	Do you have any strong feelings about my growing a beard?	a. It doesn't mind me. b. I don't care one way or the other. c. It's for you.
5.	If you'd rather I drop you off here, I will.	a. I don't feel strongly. b. It's entirely yours. c. It doesn't make any difference.
6.	Do you care whether we see a science fiction movie?	a. No. It's your decision. b. No. I don't have any feelings. c. No. It's whether or not you go.
7.	Would it disturb you if I turned on the rock music station?	a. No. I'd rather you make the decision. b. No. It's entirely disturbing. c. No. It doesn't matter to me.

InterChange

Pet Peeves!

Do people ever do things that really bother you or disturb you? Does it bother you when people talk too loudly, use bad table manners, chew gum loudly, or scratch fingernails on the blackboard? Tell about any *pet peeves* you have.

A waiter at The International Gourmet restaurant is taking someone's order. Practice this scene with a partner.

A. Welcome to The International Gourmet. My name is Walter, and I'll be your waiter this evening. Would you like to see the menu, or would you care to order our special complete dinner of the day?

B. What's the special today?

A. Leg of lamb, and I highly recommend it.

B. Well . . . let me see. I think I'll have the special.

A. All right. As an appetizer, you have a choice of fruit salad or tomato juice.

B. Hmm. I think I'd like the fruit salad.

A. All right. And the soups we're offering today are split pea or French onion.

B. Split pea or French onion? Hmm. That's a difficult choice. I guess I'd rather have the split pea.

A. And what kind of dressing would you like on your salad?

B. What do you have?

A. We have Italian, French, Russian, and blue cheese.

B. I'd prefer Italian.

A. Italian. Fine. Now, with your leg of lamb, you can have your choice of two of our side dishes. Today we're featuring brown rice, baked potato, string beans in a cream sauce, and . . . Hmm . . . Let me see if I can remember them all . . . Oh, yes. We also have fresh squash and marinated mushrooms.

B. That's quite a selection! Let's see . . . uh . . . hmm. Let me have brown rice and fresh squash.

A. Okay. I think that's it. Oh! I almost forgot. What would you like to drink with your meal?

B. I'll have a glass of mineral water.

A. All right. I'll put this order in right away, and I'll be back in a moment with some rolls and butter.

B. Thank you.

A. Welcome to _____. My name is _____, and I'll be your waiter/waitress this evening. Would you like to see the menu, or would you care to order our special complete dinner of the day?

B. What's the special today?

A. _____, and I highly recommend it.

B. Well . . . let me see. I think I'll have the special.

A. All right. As an appetizer, you have a choice of _____ or _____.

B. Hmm. I think I'd like the _____.

A. All right. And the soups we're offering today are _____ or _____.

B. _____ or _____? Hmm. That's a difficult choice. I guess I'd rather have the _____.

A. And what kind of dressing would you like on your salad?

B. What do you have?

A. We have _____, _____, _____, and _____.

B. I'd prefer _____.

A. _____. Fine. Now, with your _____, you can have your choice of two of our side dishes. Today we're featuring _____, _____, _____, and . . . Hmm . . . Let me see if I can remember them all . . . Oh, yes. We also have _____ and _____.

B. That's quite a selection! Let's see . . . uh . . . hmm. Let me have _____ and _____.

A. Okay. I think that's it. Oh! I almost forgot. What would you like to drink with your meal?

B. I'll have _____.

A. All right. I'll put this order in right away, and I'll be back in a moment with some rolls and butter.

B. Thank you.

Create an original restaurant scene with your partner. Give your restaurant a name and design a "special of the day."

Special of the Day: _____

Appetizers: _____   *Soups:* _____

_____   _____

Salad Dressings: *Side Dishes:*

_____ _____   _____ _____

_____ _____   _____ _____

_____

Now create a conversation between a waiter or waitress and a customer. You can use the model above as a guide, but feel free to adapt and expand it any way you wish.

Function Review: *Chapters 4, 5, 6*

Choose the appropriate line for Speaker A.

	A	**B**
1.	a. Would you prefer Mt. Everest? (b.) Would you be interested in climbing Mt. Everest with me? c. How do you like Mt. Everest?	No, thanks. I'm not really crazy about heights!
2.	a. I didn't hear you. b. It's too big. c. That was quite a meal!	Thanks for saying so.
3.	a. Joan is always playing loud music. b. How did you like the music? c. Could you possibly turn down the music?	It wasn't as good as I thought it would be.
4.	a. Are you with me so far? b. I'm annoyed with you. c. Would you mind repeating that?	Let me see. I think so.
5.	a. What seems to be the problem with the couch? b. How do you like this couch? c. Would you mind moving the couch?	It's just what I had in mind.
6.	a. I missed that. b. I was a little disappointed. c. How would you like me to cook your hamburger?	Oh, I don't care.
7.	a. Why don't you talk to him about it? b. Do you follow me? c. I'm furious with you!	I guess I should.
8.	a. Are you satisfied with your new job? b. Would you mind if I left work early? c. What do you think of your new job?	It's your decision.
9.	a. Which store do you want to go to? b. Where should we shop? c. Are you ready?	Whenever you want to go, it's all right with me.

In 1955, a man named Raymond Kroc entered a partnership with two brothers named McDonald. They operated a popular restaurant in California that sold food that was easy to prepare and serve quickly. Hamburgers, french fries, and cold drinks were the main items on the limited menu. Kroc opened similar eating places under the same name, *McDonald's*, and they were an instant success. He later took over the company, and today it is one of the most famous and successful *fast-food* chains in the world.

Why was his idea so successful? Probably the most significant reason was that his timing was right. In the 1950s, most married women stayed home to keep house and take care of their children. During the decade of the 1960s, the movement for equality between the sexes and an economy that required more families to have two wage-earners resulted in many women returning to the workplace. This meant that they had less time and energy to devote to housework and preparation of meals, so they relied more on *TV dinners* and fast-food restaurants.

Single parents also have little time to spend in the kitchen. Convenience foods, processed and packaged, help a great deal. People living alone because of divorce or a preference for a singles lifestyle also depend on this type of food, since cooking for one is often more trouble than it is worth. Food manufacturers have begun catering to this new market and now sell smaller portions specially prepared for one person.

Fast food, or junk food as it is sometimes called, is not part of the diet of all Americans. Another trend of the 1960s, sometimes called the back-to-nature movement, influenced many people to avoid food that was packaged or processed. More and more Americans based their diets on natural foods containing no chemicals, such as additives, preservatives, or artificial colors or flavors. This preference for natural foods continues to this day. These products can now be found not only in the special health food stores but also on the shelves of many supermarkets.

The success of Raymond Kroc's fast-food business and the increasing interest in natural foods are illustrations of the way in which social and economic trends influence where and what we eat.

In Your Own Words

For Writing and Discussion

Has the diet in your country changed much during the past thirty years?
What is your country's version of *fast food*?
When do people eat traditional dishes, and when do they eat *fast food*?

Here are the expressions you practiced in Chapter 6. Try to use as many as you can to expand your vocabulary and to add variety to your use of English.

Preference

Inquiring about . . .

Would you {
  prefer _____?
  rather have _____?
  like _____?
}

Would you like to
Would you prefer to
Would you rather   _____
Do you want to   (or _____)?
Would you care to

How would you like it?

Do you have any strong feelings
   about it?
Do you have any feelings about it one
   way or another?
Do you care one way or the other?
Do you have a preference?

Expressing . . .

I'd prefer _____.
I'd rather have _____.
I'd like _____.

I'd prefer to _____.
I'd rather _____.
I'd like to _____.
I'd much rather _____.

I'd prefer not to _____.

I feel strongly about _____ing.

If you'd rather I didn't _____, I won't.

Want–Desire

Inquiring about . . .

When do you want to _____?
Who would you like to _____?
What would you like to do?
How would you like me to _____?
Which _____ would you rather _____?
Where do you want _____ to _____?

Expressing . . .

I'd like _____.
I'll have _____.
I want _____.

I (really) don't feel like _____ing.
I'm not (really) in the mood to _____.
I'd (really) prefer not to _____.

_____ wants me to _____.

Requests

Direct, More Polite

Would you mind
Would it bother you   } if I _____ed?
Would it disturb you

Indifference

Whenever _____ is fine with me.
(Whoever . . . Whatever . . .
   However . . . Whichever . . .
   Wherever . . .)

It doesn't make any difference (to me).
It doesn't matter (to me).
It's all the same to me.
I don't care.
I don't feel strongly about it one way
   or the other.

It doesn't matter to me whether you
   _____ or not.

It's (entirely) up to you.
It's (entirely) your decision.
It's for you to decide.

Hesitating

Well . . .
Let me see . . .
Let's see . . .
Hmm . . .
Okay . . .
Uh . . .
I think . . .
I guess . . .

These scenes review the functions and conversation strategies in Chapters, 4, 5, and 6. Who do you think these people are? What do you think they're talking about? With other students, improvise conversations based on these scenes and act them out.

1.

2.

3.

4.

5.

6.

7.

8.

104

7

PROMISES
INTENTIONS

Howard and Helen are going out for a while and leaving their son in charge of the house. What do you think they're saying to each other?

Maya is talking about her future plans with her high school counselor. What do you think they're saying to each other?

(1) rely on
depend on
count on

(2) I promise I'll
I promise to

turn off the lights when you leave

A. Can I **rely on**(1) you to turn off the lights when you leave?
B. Yes. **I promise I'll**(2) turn them off.
A. You won't forget? It's really important.
B. Don't worry. You can **rely on**(1) me.

1. pick up the soda for the party tonight

2. bring back my computer tomorrow

3. drop off my suit at the cleaner's on the way to school

4. put away your toys before our guests arrive

5. clean up the kitchen before the health inspector gets here

Promise somebody you'll do something.

A. Will the car be ready by five?
B. Yes, it will.
A. Can I **depend on**(1) that?
B. **Absolutely!**(2) **I promise**(3) it'll be ready by five.
A. Okay. I'm **counting**(4) on you.
B. Don't worry! I won't **let you down.**(5)

(1) depend on
     count on
     rely on
     be sure of

(2) Absolutely!
     Definitely!
     Positively!

(3) I promise (you)
     I assure you
     I guarantee (that)
     I give you my word
     You can be sure

(4) counting
     depending
     relying

(5) let you down
     disappoint you

1.

2.

3.

4.

5.

"Extract" a promise from somebody.

Grammar Check: *Two-Word Verbs*

Choose the best preposition to form a two-word verb.

a.	rely (down out (on))		**f.**	drop (off at up)
b.	depend (in on of)		**g.**	put (on of at)
c.	pick (back down up)		**h.**	run (into of at)
d.	count (on into of)		**i.**	break (under down at)
e.	bring (of back at)		**j.**	turn (on at of)

Complete the following with the most appropriate two-word verbs from above. There may be more than one possible answer for each question.

_g_ **1.** Michael _____ his best suit for his job interview yesterday.

____ **2.** Carol called the furniture store to see when she could _____ her new sofa.

____ **3.** The president has great faith in you. He knows he can _____ you.

____ **4.** There's a great movie on tonight. Let's _____ the television.

____ **5.** I need my laptop computer back so I can type my history paper. When can you _____ it _____ to me?

____ **6.** Do you ever _____ your old friend Felix anymore?

____ **7.** You need to _____ this book _____ to the library in a week.

____ **8.** I'm afraid this old car is in bad condition. I'm really worried that it's going to _____.

Grammar Check: *WILL*

The Dawsons are very nervous parents. Their son, Danny, is about to go off to college, and they're concerned about him living away from home for the first time. What do you think they're saying to him?

A. _____?

B. Yes. I'll call you every week.

A. _____?

B. No. I won't be lonely.

A. _____?

B. Yes. I give you my word that I'll study hard.

A. _____?

B. Yes. I promise I won't get into any trouble!

A. _____?

B. Yes, Mom and Dad. I'll miss you!

Function Check: *What's the Expression?*

1. Can I _____ you to drive the car safely?
   a. guarantee
   b. depend on *(circled)*
   c. be sure

2. Don't worry! I won't _____.
   a. be sure
   b. disappoint you
   c. give you my word

3. I'll try not to _____.
   a. assure you
   b. be sure
   c. let you down

4. You can _____ depend on Bob.
   a. be sure of
   b. positive
   c. definitely

5. You should _____ your own instincts.
   a. rely on
   b. depend
   c. guarantee

6. Helen says she'll _____ me a position on the committee next year.
   a. let
   b. assure
   c. rely

Listening: *Who's Talking?*

Listen and decide what the relationship between the two speakers is.

1. a. student–teacher
   b. teenager–parent *(circled)*
   c. customer–car dealer

2. a. doctor–patient
   b. principal–student
   c. employee–employer

3. a. editor–journalist
   b. boyfriend–girlfriend
   c. judge–lawyer

4. a. passenger–taxi driver
   b. flight attendant–pilot
   c. passenger–train conductor

5. a. student–student
   b. store owner–customer
   c. computer salesman– secretary

6. a. store manager–clerk
   b. customer–cashier
   c. librarian–assistant

InterAct!

Political Promises

The Situation: Two or three people in the class are running for political office. You decide who the candidates are. The rest of the students are concerned citizens, people who live in the community. They're upset about several important issues.

The Process: Small groups of citizens work together to come up with important concerns they have. Perhaps they're economic problems, transportation problems, or issues of public safety. The groups then question the candidates, asking them to promise to make changes.

I promise . . .

I give you my word . . .

You can be sure . . .

The Conclusion: The citizens should vote for the person they consider the best candidate—the person whose promises are the most convincing!

the salesman who sold me this watch

A. I'm very **disappointed with**[1] the salesman who sold me this watch.
B. How come?
A. He guaranteed that this watch was waterproof, but it isn't!
B. **That's too bad.**[2] Are you going to talk to him about it? After all, he DID give you his word.
A. **Maybe I should.**[3]

my next-door neighbor

A. I'm very **disappointed in**[1] my next-door neighbor.
B. How come?
A. She gave me her word she would keep her dog off my lawn, but she hasn't!
B. **That's a shame.**[2] Are you going to talk to her about it? After all, she DID give you her word.
A. **I guess I will.**[3]

---

[1] disappointed with
disappointed in

[2] That's too bad.
That's a shame.
What a shame!

[3] Maybe I should.
I guess I will.
I suppose I will.

1. my upstairs neighbor

2. my landlord

3. my daughter

4. my boss

5. my employees

6. the photographer

7. my agent in Hollywood

111

Grammar Check: *Sequence of Tenses*

Complete the sentences.

This watch *is* waterproof.	He guaranteed that this watch *was* waterproof.
I *fixed* your bicycle.	She assured me she *had fixed* my bicycle.
I*'ll* water your plants.	He promised me he *would* water my plants.
I *can* repair your stove.	She gave me her word she *could* repair my stove.

1. *I'm a competent typist.*   He assured us <u>he was a competent typist</u> .

2. *I wrote back to Mr. Waterman.*   She told me ————————————.

3. *I'll fix your broken radiator.*   Our superintendent promised ——————.

4. *I won't interfere.*   My mother-in-law promised us ——————.

5. *I can easily solve that problem.*   My accountant gave me his word ——————.

6. *We were briefed by the president.*   The aides assured the press ——————.

7. *These gloves are washable.*   The sales clerk promised me ——————.

8. *I took the garbage out.*   My son gave me his word ——————.

9. *I'll pull the tooth as quickly as I can!*   My dentist assured me ——————.

Everybody on pages 110 and 111 has decided to go back and confront the people who had disappointed them!

With a partner, choose one of the situations and reenact the encounter. Present your *confrontations* to the class and have other students help you resolve the conflict if you haven't been able to do it on your own.

A warranty is the basic agreement between a buyer and a seller: the buyer gives money in exchange for an item that the seller guarantees will work. So, for example, when you buy an expensive item such as a camera, a refrigerator, or a car, you want to get your money's worth. You shop around until you find the one that best suits your needs, and you listen carefully to the salesperson's *pitch*. Chances are he or she will tell you that a certain product is the best that money can buy! A smart shopper carefully evaluates the features of a product and determines what guarantees the dealer or manufacturer offers.

This is the best camera money can buy!

When you finally purchase the item and bring it home, you should put the product warranty in a safe place in case something goes wrong. Occasionally, a company requires the customer to send in a registration card before the warranty goes into effect. Be sure to fill this out and send it in, or the company may not honor your warranty.

There are two types of warranties—*full* and *limited*. A full warranty guarantees that the manufacturer will repair or replace an item or refund the purchase price if the item is defective. A limited warranty states that the manufacturer will repair defective parts of an item, but you usually have to take it or mail it back to the manufacturer, pay labor charges, and include money for return shipping and handling costs. Both full and limited warranties have time limits, guarantee only certain parts of the product, and do not cover damage caused by neglect or misuse.

Making a big purchase is always risky business, but it is less risky if you keep these points in mind. Shop around and compare brands and prices, ask about the warranty before you buy a product, send in the registration card, and hold on to that warranty!

In Your Own Words

Choose one of the following situations and write a letter to the company. You're upset! Complain about the defective product, remind them of the terms of the warranty, and ask for a refund or replacement.

- You bought an air conditioner last month. There was a bad storm last week, and the air conditioner hasn't worked since!

- You bought a watch that was supposed to be waterproof. After you wore it on a scuba diving expedition, it stopped working!

- You bought a color TV that worked fine for the first three months. Now all the faces are green, the sky is bright purple, and you can't adjust the colors!

When you have finished writing your letter, exchange letters with a classmate. Answer your classmate's letter, telling why you will or won't honor the request!

join the army

(1) I'm going to
I'm planning to
I plan to
I intend to
I've decided to

(2) Gee!
Boy!
Wow!

(3) I've thought about it for a long time
I've given it a lot of thought
I've given it a lot of serious consideration

A. You know, . . . I've made a decision.
B. What?
A. **I'm going to**(1) join the army.
B. **Gee!**(2) Joining the army! That's a big decision!
A. I know. It is. But **I've thought about it for a long time**,(3) and I've decided it's time to do it.
B. Well, good luck!

1. get married

2. give up smoking

3. sell my house

4. quit my job

5. apply to business school

The National Star

Tell a friend about something you're planning to do.

Grammar Check: *Gerunds and Infinitives*

1. Anne and Bob intend ((to get) getting) engaged in May.

2. Judy decided (to design   designing) a new industrial robot.

3. We enjoyed (to listen   listening) to the jazz concert last night.

4. My parents are thinking of (to buy   buying) a condominium.

5. The president is preparing (to give   giving) an important speech to Congress.

6. The bird was hopping on one foot. It seemed (to be   being) hurt.

7. The thief admitted (to steal   stealing) the minivan.

8. Uncle Charlie finally agreed (to give up   giving up) eating rich desserts.

9. I believe in (to jog   jogging) every day in order to prevent heart failure.

10. Would you consider (to go   going) to a museum with me today?

11. My stockbroker expects (to see   seeing) an increase in the stock's value.

12. When the factory worker heard the 5:00 P.M. bell, he stopped (to work   working).

13. The scientist is planning (to begin   beginning) a bold new experiment.

14. The police officer denied (to accept   accepting) a bribe.

15. My doctor suggested (to take   taking) a vacation.

16. The prisoner hopes (to get out   getting out) of jail within a few months.

Talk with a partner about an important decision each of you has had to make.

What did you have to decide?
How long did you think about it?
What were the *pros* and the *cons* (the positive and the negative factors)?
Did you ask other people's advice? What did they say?
What did you finally decide to do?
Are you pleased with your decision? Why or why not?

Then tell the class about your partner's important decision.

stay home and read a book
go fishing

A. Hi! It's me!
B. Oh, hi! How are you?
A. Fine. Tell me, what are you doing this afternoon?
B. **I'm not sure.**(1) I'll **probably**(2) stay home and read a book. How about you?
A. Well, I'm planning to go fishing. **Would you like to join me?**(3)
B. Sure. **I'd be happy to.**(4) Going fishing sounds a lot more **exciting**(5) than staying home and reading a book.
A. Good! I'll pick you up at around one o'clock.
B. See you then.

(1) I'm not sure.
I'm not certain.
I don't know yet.

(2) probably
most likely

(3) Would you like to join
    me?
Do you want to join me?
Would you be interested
    in joining me?

(4) I'd be happy to.
I'd love to.
I'd like that.

(5) exciting
enjoyable
interesting

1. work in the garden
   play tennis

2. work on my car
   go swimming

3. do some chores around
      the house
   see the new exhibit at
      the museum

4. work on my term paper
   see a movie

5. catch up on some work at
      the office
   play a few rounds of golf

Respond to a friend's invitation.

Function Check: *What's My Line?*

Choose the appropriate line for Speaker B.

	A		**B**

1. Pam, what are you doing tonight?
   a. I'd be happy to.
   b. I'm not likely.
   c. I don't know yet. *(circled)*

2. Would you like to join me in going to a rock concert?
   a. Sure. I'd be exciting.
   b. Thanks. I'd love to.
   c. Sure. I'm like that.

3. Does the show start at 9:00 or 10:00?
   a. I'm not certain.
   b. I'm probably sure.
   c. It's most likely.

4. Would you be interested in going scuba diving with me?
   a. Sure. Going scuba diving sounds exciting.
   b. Sure. I'm certainly going to.
   c. Sure. I'd most likely love to do that.

5. Do you want to see the new exhibit at the Museum of Modern Art?
   a. Yes. I'm interesting.
   b. I like enjoyable.
   c. I'd like that.

6. Are you doing anything special this afternoon?
   a. I'll most likely do some errands.
   b. I'd love to.
   c. Good! Pick me up around 2:00.

Listening: *The Best Response*

Listen and choose the best response.

1. a. How about you?
   b. Oh, hi! How's everything? *(circled)*
   c. Fine.

2. a. Fine, thanks.
   b. I'd love to.
   c. I'm not sure.

3. a. I'm going to read a book.
   b. I don't know yet.
   c. I'm going to be fine.

4. a. Good. I'll be interested.
   b. Okay. I'll see you then.
   c. I'll most likely be there.

5. a. Well, I'm not.
   b. Good!
   c. Sure, I'd be happy to.

6. a. See you then.
   b. That sounds like fun.
   c. Would you like to join me?

(1) I've been thinking of
I'm thinking of
I've been thinking about
I'm thinking about

(2) I thought I might
I thought I'd
I might
I may

A. Have you decided who you're going to ask to the prom?
B. No. I haven't made up my mind yet. **I've been thinking of** (1) asking Susan, but then again, **I thought I might** (2) ask Elizabeth.
A. Sounds like a difficult decision. I'll be curious to know what you decide.
B. I'll let you know.
A. Promise?
B. Promise.

1. Chemistry
   Music

2. to Florida
   to Arizona

3. right away
   when business gets better

4. on our next date
   in a long letter

5. an IBM
   a Macintosh

Talk with a friend about a difficult decision.

Listening: *Definite, Probable, or Possible?*

Listen to the conversation and decide whether Speaker B's plan of action is *definite*, *probable*, or *possible*.

1. a. definite
   b. probable
   (c.) possible

2. a. definite
   b. probable
   c. possible

3. a. definite
   b. probable
   c. possible

4. a. definite
   b. probable
   c. possible

5. a. definite
   b. probable
   c. possible

6. a. definite
   b. probable
   c. possible

7. a. definite
   b. probable
   c. possible

8. a. definite
   b. probable
   c. possible

9. a. definite
   b. probable
   c. possible

Listening: *What's the Meaning?*

Listen and choose the answer that is closest in meaning to the sentence you have heard.

1. a. I'm going to make an apple pie tonight.
   b. Tonight's dessert is apple pie.
   (c.) I may make an apple pie for dessert.

2. a. I'm not taking Chinese.
   b. I'm thinking of studying Chinese.
   c. I'm learning Chinese.

3. a. I made my father a sweater for his birthday.
   b. My father thought I made him a sweater for his birthday.
   c. I'm thinking of making a sweater for my father's birthday.

4. a. I might leave early today.
   b. I made him go home early today.
   c. May I go home early today?

5. a. Ruth might ask me to the prom.
   b. I think Ruth asked me to the prom.
   c. I might ask Ruth to the prom.

6. a. I want to change my major.
   b. I'm thinking of changing my job.
   c. I've decided to change my job.

InterCultural Connections

The people in Situation 2 on page 118 are talking about their retirement. One says he might move to Florida or possibly to Arizona, two warm-weather spots where many older Americans spend their retirement years.

What about people in your country? At what age do people typically retire from their jobs, and what do they usually do?

How about you? What do you think you'll do when YOU retire?

I'll probably . . .

I may . . .

I thought I might . . .

I'll definitely . . .

Imagine what you'll do, and share your thoughts with your classmates.

do Room 407

(1) I was planning to
I was going to
I intended to
I thought I would

(2) a little later
in a little while

(3) right away
right now
as soon as I can
the first chance I get

A. Have you done Room 407 yet?
B. No, I haven't. **I was planning to**(1) do it **a little later.**(2)
A. Would you mind doing it soon?
B. No, not at all. I'll do it **right away.**(3)
A. Thanks.

1. write the monthly report

2. copy my memo

3. distribute the mail

4. make my hotel reservations in Chicago

5. give out the paychecks

Ask somebody to do something now, not later.

Function Check: *What's the Expression?*

1. I don't mind leaving now. I'll take you home
   _____.
   a. in a little while
   (b.) right away
   c. the first chance I get

2. I'll do my taxes _____.
   a. as soon
   b. the first chance
   c. right away

3. I _____ wash the dishes after dinner.
   a. was planning to
   b. thought of
   c. intend

4. The brownies should be checked _____.
   a. a little while
   b. a little later
   c. a while

5. I'll pick up the tickets _____.
   a. the first chance I got
   b. as soon as I can
   c. in a little later

6. I _____ to mail the letter yesterday, but I forgot to buy stamps.
   a. am planning
   b. intend
   c. was planning

7. I _____ clean up my room in a few minutes.
   a. was going
   b. intended
   c. thought I would

8. I _____ wait until tomorrow to call my insurance agent about the car.
   a. am thinking of
   b. was thinking to
   c. thought I would

InterAct!

With a partner, create a role play based on the following situation and then present it to the class.

You're a supervisor somewhere — in an office, in a restaurant, at a police station, on a movie set, or maybe at the White House! You decide where. Make a list of ten tasks you would expect an employee at that place to have done, and check to see whether or not your employee has done them.

You're the employee. Your supervisor is checking to see if you have completed your tasks. You've already done some of them, and you're planning to do others a little later. Explain to your supervisor.

Now switch roles! This time the supervisor is the employee, and the employee is the supervisor. Discuss with other students: How does it feel to be a supervisor? How does it feel to be an employee?

Two old friends who haven't seen each other in a long time bump into each other on the street. Practice this scene with a partner.

A. Well, if it isn't David Johnson!
B. Richard Peters! It's nice to see you again!
A. You know, David, I've been meaning to call you for a long time.
B. Me, too. How have you been?
A. Fine. How about yourself?
B. Pretty good.
A. Tell me, David. The last time I saw you, you were planning to go to law school, weren't you?
B. Yes, I guess I was. But as it turned out, I changed my mind.
A. Oh, really? But **if I remember correctly,**[1] you were intent on going to law school. Whatever made you change your mind?
B. Well, it's a long story, and I don't want to bore you with all the details. But **what it boils down to is that**[2] I decided that going to law school wasn't a very good idea. I decided to go to medical school instead.
A. Medical school? That's very interesting.
B. And how about you? The last time we talked, didn't you tell me you were going to open your own real estate business?
A. That's right. I was. But things turned out differently.
B. But you seemed so determined to do that. What happened?
A. Well, it's very complicated, and I'm sure you don't want to know all the details. But **as it turned out,**[2] I decided that opening my own real estate company just wasn't for me. So I decided to stay at my old job instead.
B. Well, **a lot sure has happened**[3] since we last saw each other.
A. **I'll say!**[4] You know, we should try to stay in touch.
B. Yes, we should. Let's have lunch together sometime soon.
A. Good idea.
B. Take care now.
A. You, too.

122

A. Well, if it isn't _____ _____!
B. _____ _____! It's nice to see you again!
A. You know, _____, I've been meaning to call you for a long time.
B. Me, too. How have you been?
A. Fine. How about yourself?
B. Pretty good.
A. Tell me, _____. The last time I saw you, you were planning to _____, weren't you?
B. Yes, I guess I was. But as it turned out, I changed my mind.
A. Oh, really? But **if I remember correctly,**(1) you were intent on _____ing. Whatever made you change your mind?
B. Well, it's a long story, and I don't want to bore you with all the details. But **what it boils down to is that**(2) I decided that _____ing wasn't a very good idea. I decided to _____ instead.
A. _____? That's very interesting.
B. And how about you? The last time we talked, didn't you tell me you were going to _____?
A. That's right. I was. But things turned out differently.
B. But you seemed so determined to do that. What happened?
A. Well, it's very complicated, and I'm sure you don't want to know all the details. But **as it turned out,**(2) I decided that _____ing just wasn't for me. So I decided to _____ instead.
B. Well, **a lot sure has happened**(3) since we last saw each other.
A. **I'll say!**(4) You know, we should try to stay in touch.
B. Yes, we should. Let's have lunch together sometime soon.
A. Good idea.
B. Take care now.
A. You, too.

Now create an original scene with your partner. You are two old friends who have just bumped into each other. You can use the model above as a guide, but feel free to adapt and expand it any way you wish.

Function Check: *What's My Line?*

Choose the appropriate line for Speaker B.

	A	**B**
1.	What are you doing this afternoon?	a. You can depend on me. b. I'd love to. ⓒ I've been thinking of going to the beach.
2.	Do you promise to do your homework soon?	a. I'd like that. b. Absolutely. c. I agree.
3.	I'm going out for a walk. Would you like to join me?	a. I'd be happy to. b. I give you my word. c. I've thought about it for a long time.
4.	I'm very disappointed with my new job.	a. That's too bad. b. Can I depend on that? c. Promise?
5.	Can I depend on you to call me tomorrow?	a. You're right. b. I give you my word. c. I'll say!
6.	Well, if it isn't Audrey Winston!	a. Well, it isn't! b. You can say that again! c. Melanie Peters! How nice to see you!
7.	What happened?	a. It boils down to that. b. It's a long story! c. My memory serves me correctly.
8.	I've been meaning to contact you.	a. You, too. b. Me, too. c. And you?
9.	If I remember correctly, you were intent on becoming a pilot.	a. If I recall, you were. b. As it turned out, you did. c. The fact of the matter is, I was.

Grammar Check: *Tense Review*

1. Hi, Scott! How _____ been?
   a. had you
   (b.) have you
   c. are you

2. Last time I saw you, you _____ to become a musician.
   a. plan
   b. were planning
   c. have been planning

3. I _____ I was a dreamer.
   a. guessed
   b. was guessing
   c. guess

4. About four years ago, I _____ to become a doctor.
   a. have decided
   b. will have decided
   c. decided

5. I _____ you said you were going to become a movie star.
   a. have thought
   b. thought
   c. am thinking

6. Well, my new idea is that I _____ go into financial consulting.
   a. have gone to
   b. am going to
   c. will go to

7. A lot _____ since we last met.
   a. have happened
   b. has happened
   c. is happening

8. Yes. We _____ lunch together soon.
   a. should have
   b. should have had
   c. shouldn't have

InterCultural Connections

As Richard Peters and David Johnson begin their good-byes, they say . . .

Richard: You know, we should try to stay in touch.

David: Yes, we should. Let's have lunch together sometime soon.

Richard: Good idea.

David: Take care now.

Richard: You, too.

This scene is quite typical in the United States. "Let's have lunch together sometime soon" is a common way of ending such a conversation. What's your opinion? Are these people sincere? Do you think they really mean what they say? How would this conversation take place in YOUR country?

In Your Own Words

For Writing and Discussion

Write a letter to a friend. A lot has happened since you last saw each other. Tell about it.

Now exchange letters with another student in the class. Imagine you are the friend that student wrote to. Write back to your friend.

Here are the expressions you practiced in Chapter 7. Try to use as many as you can to expand your vocabulary and to add variety to your use of English.

Intention

Inquiring about . . .

Have you decided _____?

What are you doing *this afternoon*?

Expressing . . .

I'm going to _____.
I'm planning to _____.
I plan to _____.
I intend to _____.
I've decided to _____.

I'll _____
$\begin{cases} \text{right away.} \\ \text{right now.} \\ \text{as soon as I can.} \\ \text{the first chance I get.} \end{cases}$

I've been thinking of _____ing.
I'm thinking of _____ing.
I've been thinking about _____ing.
I'm thinking about _____ing.

I've been meaning to _____ (for a long time).

I've thought about it for a long time.
I've given it a lot of thought.
I've given it a lot of serious consideration.

I've decided it's time to do it.

I haven't made up my mind yet.

I was planning to _____.
I was going to _____.
I intended to _____.
I thought I would _____.

I was intent on _____ing.
I was determined to _____.

Promising

Asking for a Promise

Can I $\begin{cases} \text{rely on} \\ \text{depend on} \\ \text{count on} \end{cases}$ you to _____?

Can I $\begin{cases} \text{depend on} \\ \text{count on} \\ \text{rely on} \\ \text{be sure of} \end{cases}$ that?

Promise?

Offering a Promise

Promise.
I promise I'll _____.
I promise to _____.

I promise (you) _____.
I assure you _____.
I guarantee (that) _____.
I give you my word _____.
You can be sure _____.

Absolutely.
Definitely.
Positively.

You can $\begin{cases} \text{rely on} \\ \text{depend on} \\ \text{count on} \end{cases}$ me.

I won't let you down.
I won't disappoint you.

Invitations

Extending . . .

Would you like to join me?
Do you want to join me?
Would you be interested in joining me?

Accepting . . .

I'd be happy to.
I'd love to.
I'd like that.

Disappointment

I'm (very) disappointed with/in _____.

Sympathizing

That's too bad.
That's a shame.
What a shame!

Surprise-Disbelief

Gee!
Boy!
Wow!

Certainty/Uncertainty

Expressing Uncertainty

I'm not sure.
I'm not certain.
I don't know yet.

Probability/Improbability

Expressing Probability

I'll probably _____.
I'll most likely _____.

Possibility/Impossibility

Expressing Possibility

I might _____.
I may _____.
I thought I might _____.
I thought I'd _____.

Agreement/Disagreement

Expressing Agreement

I agree.
You're right.
I'll say!
You can say that again!

Initiating Conversations

Hi! It's me!

Well, if it isn't _____!

Initiating a Topic

You know . . .

Focusing Attention

What it boils down to is that . . .
The fact of the matter is that . . .
As it turned out, . . .

8

OFFERING HELP
GRATITUDE AND
APPRECIATION

Shirley is setting up the conference room for a meeting. Her co-worker, Doris, is offering to help. What do you think they're saying to each other?

Ted is a salesperson at Video City Electronics. He's helping a customer select a TV. What do you think they're saying to each other?

Do You Want Me to Wash the Dishes?

wash the dishes

A. **Do you want me to**[1] wash the dishes?
B. No. **Don't worry about it.**[2] I don't mind washing them.
A. **No, really!**[3] You're always the one who washes the dishes.
   Let me, **for a change.**[4]
B. Okay. Thanks. **I appreciate it.**[5]

[1] Do you want me to _____?
    Would you like me to _____?
    I'll _____, if you'd like.
    I'll be happy/glad to _____,
       if you'd like.
    I'd be happy/glad to _____,
       if you'd like.

[2] Don't worry about it.
    That's okay/all right.

[3] No, really!
    Listen!
    (Oh,) come on!

[4] for a change
    for once

[5] I appreciate it/that.
    I'd appreciate it/that.
    It's (very) nice/kind of you
       to offer.
    That's (very) nice/kind of you.
    That would be nice.

1. water the plants

2. mow the lawn

3. take out the garbage

4. defrost the refrigerator

5. feed the hamster

Offer to do something for somebody.

Want Any Help?

change the oil

A. I see you're changing the oil.
B. Yes. It hasn't been changed in a long time.
A. **Want any help?**[1]
B. Sure. **If you don't mind.**[2]
A. No, not at all. **I'd be happy to give you a hand.**[3]
B. Thanks. I appreciate it.

[1] (Do you) want any help?
(Do you) need any help?
(Do you) want a hand?
(Do you) need a hand?
Can I help?
Can I give you a hand?

[2] If you don't mind.
If you wouldn't mind.
If it's no trouble.

[3] I'd be happy/glad to give
you a hand.
I'd be happy/glad to lend
a hand.
I'd be happy/glad to help.

1. clean the garage

2. wash the windows

3. paint the fence

4. sweep out the barn

5. shampoo Rover

Offer to help
somebody.

129

Function Check: *What's My Line?*

Choose the appropriate line for Speaker B.

	A	**B**
1.	Do you want me to sweep the floor?	a. For a change. b. That's nice. c. No. That's all right. *(circled)*
2.	Oh, no! I'm late, and I still haven't walked the dog!	a. Do you want me? b. I'll be glad. c. I'll be glad to walk him, if you'd like.
3.	Would you like me to type that for you?	a. No. Listen! b. No. Don't worry about it. c. No. That's not nice.
4.	Let me do the laundry for once. You're always doing it.	a. Okay. That would be very nice of you. b. Okay. I'd appreciate that offer. c. Okay. Don't worry about it.
5.	Thank you for offering, Tom, but I don't mind vacuuming.	a. No, really! I'd appreciate that. b. No! Come! You're always vacuuming. c. No, really! You're always the one who vacuums.

Listening: *Conclusions*

Listen and choose the best conclusion.

1. a. Mrs. Crawford and Sally are driving in a car.
   b. Mrs. Crawford and Sally are closing the store at the end of the day. *(circled)*
   c. Mrs. Crawford and Sally are opening the store at the beginning of the day.

2. a. Bob and Mike are going to drive to work together.
   b. Bob and Mike don't like to drive to work together.
   c. Bob and Mike are not going to drive together today.

3. a. Richard always feeds the baby.
   b. Richard is going to change the baby.
   c. Richard is going to feed the baby.

4. a. John doesn't want Linda to go shopping.
   b. John doesn't like shopping.
   c. John wants Linda to go shopping.

5. a. Mr. Jones is glad Jack will write the memo.
   b. Jack is not going to write the memo.
   c. Mr. Jones is not going to write the memo.

Listen and choose the best response.

1. a. Sure. I'd be glad to.
    b. Sure. I can give you a hand.
    c. Sure. If it's no trouble.

2. a. If you wouldn't mind.
    b. No, if you mind.
    c. No trouble.

3. a. Yes. I'd be happy.
    b. No. I'd appreciate it.
    c. No. I'd be glad to lend a hand.

4. a. Thanks. It's nice of you to offer.
    b. Thanks. I'd be happy to.
    c. Thanks. I'd be glad to lend a hand.

5. a. Sure. If you don't mind.
    b. Sure. If you mind.
    c. Sure. If I don't mind.

6. a. Oh, come on!
    b. No. That's okay.
    c. Sure. Don't mind.

7. a. Well, do you need a hand?
    b. Well, can I give something?
    c. Well, do you mind any help?

8. a. I'd be glad to trouble you.
    b. Can I hand it to you?
    c. Do you want a hand?

9. a. Thanks. If it wouldn't mind.
    b. Thanks. If it's no trouble.
    c. Thanks. You would be nice.

10. a. It's no trouble.
    b. You don't mind.
    c. Do you want a hand?

InterView

Household Chores

Take a survey of students in the class to find out who does the daily chores in their households.
Find out . . .

Who washes the dishes?	Who takes out the garbage?	Who cleans the yard?
Who dries the dishes?	Who makes the bed?	Who washes the windows?
Who dusts the furniture?	Who does the laundry?	Who repairs things around
Who sweeps the floor?	Who irons?	the house?
Who vacuums the rug?	Who mows the lawn?	Who feeds the pets?

Discuss the survey results with the class:
Do men and women share the household chores equally?
Which chores are not shared equally?

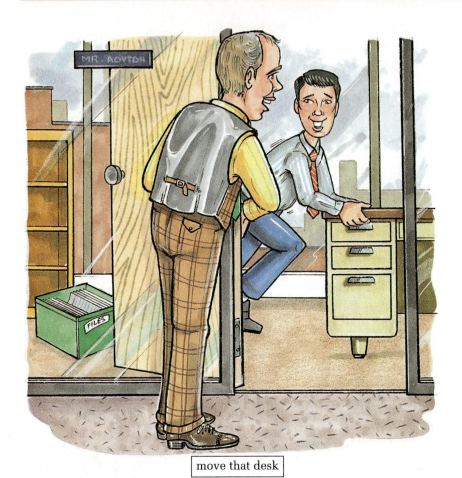

move that desk

A. **Would you like me to help you**[1] move that desk?
B. No, that's okay. I can move it myself.
A. Oh, come on! Let me give you a hand. **There's no sense in your**[2] moving it yourself if I'm here to help.
B. Really, **it's nice of you to offer,**[3] but . . .
A. **Look!**[4] I insist! You're not moving that desk by yourself!
B. Well, okay. But I really don't want to **trouble you.**[5]
A. No trouble at all! Honestly! I'm happy to lend a hand.

[1] Would you like me to
    help you _____?
Do you want me to help
    you _____?
I'd be happy/glad to help
    you _____, (if you'd
    like).
Let me help you _____.
Would you like any help
    _____ing?
Would you like me to
    give you a hand
    _____ing?

[2] There's no sense in your
    _____ing
There's no reason (for
    you) to _____
You don't have to
    _____
You shouldn't have to
    _____

[3] it's nice of you to offer
thanks for offering
I appreciate your offering

[4] Look!
Listen!
Come on!

[5] trouble you
bother you
inconvenience you
put you to any trouble
put you out

1. lift that motor

2. carry those boxes

132

3. take down that sign

4. unload that truck

5. set those chairs up

6. cut that tree down

7. adjust that TV antenna

8. change that tire

9. alphabetize those index cards

Insist on helping somebody.

133

Function Check: *What's the Expression?*

1. _____ help you put up those posters?
   a. Do you want to
   b. Do you want me to *(circled)*
   c. Would you like to

2. Really. _____ of you to offer, but I'll fix my bike by myself.
   a. Thanks
   b. I'm glad
   c. It's nice

3. _____! I insist on helping you load the truck.
   a. Help
   b. Come on
   c. Thanks

4. Well, if you insist! But I really don't want to _____.
   a. bother
   b. put you anywhere
   c. trouble you

5. There's no _____ for you to carry that computer by yourself!
   a. sense
   b. reason
   c. help

6. Would you like _____ cutting that wood?
   a. any help
   b. me to
   c. me to help

7. Oh. That's okay, but _____.
   a. I appreciate
   b. it's nice of you to offer
   c. there's no bother

8. If you really want to help, you can, but I don't want _____.
   a. to put you in
   b. to inconvenience you
   c. to bother me

Listening: *What's the Meaning?*

Listen and choose the answer that is closest in meaning to the sentence you have heard.

1. a. Let me carry those books for you, Fred. *(circled)*
   b. It's nice of you to offer to carry those books, Fred.
   c. Fred, give me those books!

2. a. I accept your offer of help.
   b. That's okay. I can do it myself.
   c. Come on! I need your help.

3. a. Look at this dirty basement!
   b. Look! Your sister wants to help you clean the basement.
   c. Look! I'm going to help you clean the basement!

4. a. I want some help with the positioning of that picture.
   b. I'm happy I could help you with the positioning of that picture.
   c. Let me help you adjust the position of that picture.

5. a. All right. But I don't want to inconvenience you.
   b. All right. Help me, but don't bother me.
   c. Thanks, but I don't want you to get into trouble.

6. a. Oh, no! You're in trouble. Lend me a hand.
   b. It's not inconvenient for me. I'm glad to help you.
   c. Oh, I'm not too happy about troubling you.

7. a. Chopping all those carrots doesn't make any sense.
   b. There's no reason for you to chop carrots.
   c. You shouldn't have to chop all those carrots by yourself.

Classroom Drama: *Offering Help!*

With a group of students, prepare a role play based on the following situation and act it out.

- Somebody is trying to do something, but is having trouble.

- A friend/neighbor/co-worker comes along and offers to help.

- The first person accepts the offer of help, but the two people are still having difficulty.

- A third person comes along, offers help, and assists the others.

- There are still problems, and more people come by, offer assistance, and attempt to help.

You decide what the problem is . . . and how it gets solved. When you're ready, present your *classroom drama*.

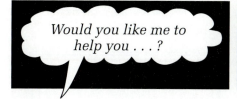

Would you like me to help you . . . ?

I'd be glad to help you . . . .

I insist! You shouldn't have to . . .

Offer to help several people you know and see how they respond to your offer.

How many people accept your offer? What do they say?
How many people refuse your offer? What do they say?
What does this tell you about people's willingness to accept assistance?

Tell about where you live:

Is it common for neighbors to offer to do things for each other?
How about co-workers or friends?

135

a digital watch

(1) May I help you?
Can I help you?

(2) Is there anything/ something in particular I can help you find?
Is there anything/ something you're looking for in particular?

(3) please let me know if I can be of any further assistance
please feel free to call on me if I can be of any further assistance
if I can be of any further assistance, please don't hesitate to ask/let me know

A. **May I help you?**(1)
B. Not right now, thanks. I'm just looking.
A. **Is there anything in particular I can help you find?**(2)
B. Well, actually, I'm looking for a digital watch.
A. Oh, I'm afraid we don't have any more digital watches in stock, but we expect some in very soon. Is there anything else I can help you with?
B. I guess not. But thanks anyway.
A. Well, **please let me know if I can be of any further assistance.**(3)
B. Thanks very much.

1. a size 40 jacket

2. a convertible sofa-bed

3. size 34 underwear

4. a remote-control VCR

5. sugar-free chewing gum

Offer to help a customer in a store.

Function Check: *What's My Line?*

Choose the appropriate line for Speaker A.

	A	**B**
1.	a. Are you just looking? b. Can I help look? c. May I assist you? *(circled)*	No, not right now, thanks. I'm just looking.
2.	a. Is there something in gold? b. Is there anything in particular I can help you find? c. Are you looking for a gold tie clip?	Well, I'm actually looking for a gold tie clip.
3.	a. Please let me know if I can be of any further assistance. b. If I can't assist you, please hesitate to call me. c. Please feel free to assist me.	Okay. Thanks very much.
4.	a. Is there any further assistance? b. Is there anything in particular? c. Is there anything else I can help you with?	I guess not, but thanks anyway.
5.	a. We're out of convertibles. Sorry. b. I'm afraid we don't have any more convertibles. Try our other store. c. We've run out of convertibles, but we expect some by the end of the week.	Okay. I'll come back then.

Listening: *What's the Answer?*

Listen carefully for specific details and answer the question at the end of each conversation.

1. a. a word processor for her father's birthday next week.
    b. a food processor for her father's birthday next week
    c. a food processor for her father's birthday tomorrow *(circled)*

2. a. size 13 brown leather shoes
    b. size 30 black leather shoes
    c. size 13 black leather shoes

3. a. He wants the exercise.
    b. He wants to change the dog's habits.
    c. He wants to do Patty a favor.

4. a. Flexible Flyers aren't made anymore.
    b. The customer was at the wrong store.
    c. The stockroom of the store was empty.

5. a. birds
    b. dogs, cats, fish, and birds
    c. dogs, cats, fish, and hamsters

6. a. in a florist shop
    b. in Vicky's backyard
    c. in Vicky's house

A. Excuse me. Are you **okay**?[1]
B. Well, uh . . . I'm not sure.
A. What happened?
B. I was knocked down by someone on rollerblades!
A. Oh, no! **Can I do anything to help?**[2]
B. No, that's okay. I think I'll be all right.
A. Well, here. **Let me**[3] help you up.
B. Thanks. **You're very kind.**[4]
A. **Don't mention it.**[5]

[1] okay
all right

[2] Can I do anything to help?
Is there anything I can do to help?
Can I help?

[3] Let me
Allow me to

[4] You're very kind/nice.
That's (very) kind/nice of you.

[5] Don't mention it.
You're welcome.
Glad to be of help.
No problem.

1.

2.

3.

4.

5.

Offer to help a stranger who has been hurt.

Function Check: *What's the Expression?*

1. Excuse me. Are you _____?
   a. very kind
   b. okay (circled)
   c. helped

2. Can I _____ to help?
   a. anything
   b. do
   c. do anything

3. I was _____ by someone!
   a. fainted
   b. mugged
   c. sprained

4. Glad to _____.
   a. do help
   b. mention it
   c. be of help

5. Here. Let me _____.
   a. to help you.
   b. allow you
   c. help you up

6. Thanks. You're _____.
   a. very kind
   b. kind of you
   c. nice of you

7. Don't _____.
   a. be glad to help
   b. mention it
   c. problem

8. Is there _____ to help?
   a. something
   b. anything I can do
   c. no problem

Vocabulary Check: *"Out of Place"*

Which word does not relate to the rest of the words in the group?

1. a. rollerblades   b. car   c. bus   d. truck driver (circled)
2. a. ankle   b. knee   c. wrinkle d. thigh
3. a. mugged   b. arrested c. robbed   d. murdered
4. a. welcome   b. kind   c. helpful d. nice
5. a. sprained   b. strained c. fell   d. injured

InterChange

Personal Experiences

The people on page 138 had some very unfortunate experiences. Has anything like that ever happened to you?

What happened?
Were you hurt?
Was someone else hurt?
Did anybody offer to help?

Talk with a partner about your experiences. Then re-enact the scene for the rest of the class.

lend me your calculator

A. You know, I keep forgetting to thank you for lending me your calculator.
B. Oh, **it was nothing.**(1)
A. **No, I mean it!**(2) It was very nice of you to lend it to me. **I'm very grateful to you.**(3)
B. **I'm glad I could do it.**(4)

1. loan me your car

2. give me a promotion

3. send me flowers when I was in the hospital

4. create a new position at the company for my daughter

5. fix my son up with your niece

Express your gratitude and appreciation to somebody.

Function Check: *What's My Line?*

Choose the appropriate line for Speaker B.

A	**B**
1. Thank you so much for lending me your portable TV.	a. Oh. It wasn't mentioned. b. (Oh. It was nothing.) *[circled]* c. Oh. No mention.
2. Really! It was nice of you to help me.	a. It was my doing. b. I'm glad I could do it. c. Any pleasure.
3. You can borrow my tape recorder whenever you wish.	a. I'm very appreciate. b. Thank you. I'm really very much. c. I really appreciate it.
4. You don't have to thank me. It was my pleasure to show you around the city.	a. No, honestly! It was very nice of you. b. No. You're nice. c. No. I mean it! You're grateful!
5. Thank you so much for your hospitality. I really enjoyed myself.	a. Any time. b. My help. c. I'm helpful.

Grammar Check: *Indirect Objects*

1. The boss was so happy that she _____.
   a. gave to him a promotion
   b. (gave him a promotion) *[circled]*
   c. gave a promotion for him

2. When are you going to _____ a new pair of sneakers?
   a. buy her
   b. buy for her
   c. buy to her

3. Excuse me, Mrs. Black. Could you please _____?
   a. pass for me the salt
   b. pass to me the salt
   c. pass me the salt

4. My supervisor _____ a wonderful recommendation.
   a. wrote me
   b. wrote to me
   c. wrote for me

5. When we were young, my father used to _____ bedtime stories.
   a. tell to us
   b. tell us
   c. tell for us

6. I needed to borrow a laptop computer, and my roommate _____.
   a. lent me mine
   b. lent hers to me
   c. lent me her

InterCultural Connections

In Situation 5 on page 140, one person is thanking the other for arranging a date for his son. Although it's most common in the United States for two people to meet on their own, occasionally friends or relatives arrange dates. Marriages in the United States are almost never pre-arranged. What about in your country? How do people usually meet each other? Are dates ever arranged by other people? Are marriages ever pre-arranged?

A movie star is accepting an award. Practice this acceptance speech.

I'm very grateful to receive this award for *Best Actress*. I can't begin to tell you how much I appreciate this honor. There are many people I'd like to thank.

First of all,[1] I want to thank my parents for bringing me into this world.

I also want to express my gratitude to all of my teachers over the years, but especially to my acting teacher, Vincent Lewis, who taught me everything I know.

And finally, I want to express my appreciation to all of my friends for their **support,**[2] especially to Katherine Miller, for being there when I needed her.

This award means a great deal to me. Words can't express how **honored**[3] I feel at this moment. Thank you very much.

[1] First of all,	[2] support	[3] honored
First and foremost,	encouragement	thrilled
Most of all,	help	excited
Above all,	advice	proud
	assistance	overwhelmed
	guidance	
	inspiration	

I'm very grateful to receive this award for _____.
I can't begin to tell you how much I appreciate this honor.
There are many people I'd like to thank.

First of all,[1] I want to thank my parents for _____.

I also want to express my gratitude to all of my teachers over the years, but especially to _____, who _____.

And finally, I want to express my appreciation to all of my friends for their _____,[2] especially to _____, for _____.

This award means a great deal to me. Words can't express how _____[3] I feel at this moment. Thank you very much.

You have also just received an award! Create an acceptance speech. You can use the model above as a guide, but feel free to adapt and expand it any way you wish.

Oscar, Emmy, Grammy, Tony—these sound like names of people, but actually they are awards given to entertainers in the United States every year. Each of these award ceremonies is a gala affair, usually held in Hollywood or New York. Hundreds of would-be winners dress in formal attire to triumphantly accept their prize or graciously acknowledge others who win.

The oldest of these awards is the Oscar, a small statue presented by the Academy of Motion Picture Arts and Sciences. The Academy Awards ceremony originated in 1928 in Hollywood to honor outstanding achievement in performance, photography, direction, production, music, and other areas of film-making. The name Oscar was supposedly given to the small statue in 1931 when the librarian and, later, executive director of the Academy, Margaret Herrick, remarked that it looked like her Uncle Oscar.

The Emmy is presented by the National Academy for Television Arts and Sciences to the top programs, performers, and behind-the-scenes people in commercial and public television. The Grammy is awarded by the national Academy of Recording Arts and Sciences and honors a variety of singers, musicians, producers, writers, technicians, and the music they have produced.

The Tony is an award that pays tribute to outstanding achievement in the theater. It was first presented in 1947 and named for a then-popular actress, Antoinette Perry. It honors the best among Broadway dramas and musicals in categories similar to those of the Oscar.

Millions of viewers watch these award ceremonies on television and are overjoyed when their favorite stars receive a prize. The candidates themselves spend weeks planning what they will wear, who they will go with, and what they will say in their acceptance speeches. Hundreds of thousands of dollars are spent on an event that is over in just a few hours. The winners take the coveted prizes home, grateful for the recognition their talent and hard work have brought them. The losers smile graciously, express how happy they are for the winners, and think to themselves, "Next year will be my turn!"

In Your Own Words

For Writing and Discussion

Imagine that you're a journalist! Your newspaper has assigned you to cover an award ceremony. Write an article describing the awards given, who won them, what the winners said in their acceptance speeches, who else was present at the event, and what people wore.

Here are the expressions you practiced in Chapter 8. Try to use as many as you can to expand your vocabulary and to add variety to your use of English.

Offering to Do Something

Do you want me to _____?
Would you like me to _____?
I'll _____, if you'd like.
I'll be happy/glad to _____, if you'd like.
I'd be happy/glad to _____, if you'd like.

Let me (_____).

Offering to Help

Making an Offer

(Do you) want any help?
(Do you) need any help?
(Do you) want a hand?
(Do you) need a hand?
Can I help?
Can I give you a hand?

Would you like me to help you _____?
Do you want me to help you _____?
I'd be glad/happy to help you _____, (if you'd like).
Let me help you _____.
Would you like any help _____ing?
Would you like me to give you a hand _____ing?

Can I do anything to help?
Is there anything I can do to help?
Can I help?

I'd be happy/glad to give you a hand.
I'd be happy/glad to lend a hand.
I'd be happy/glad to help.

Let me give you a hand.
I'm happy to lend a hand.

Let me _____.
Allow me to _____.

May I help you?
Can I help you?

Is there anything/something in particular I can help you find?
Is there anything/something you're looking for in particular?

Is there anything else I can help you with?

Please let me know if I can be of any further assistance.
Please feel free to call on me if I can be of any further assistance.
If I can be of any further assistance, please don't hesitate to ask/let me know.

Responding to an Offer

If you don't mind.
If you wouldn't mind.
If it's no trouble.

I don't want to { trouble you. / bother you. / inconvenience you. / put you to any trouble. / put you out. }

Don't worry about it.
That's okay/all right.

Gratitude

Expressing . . .

Thanks (very much).
Thank you (very much).

I'm very grateful (to _____).

I want to thank _____.
I want to express my gratitude to _____.

I keep forgetting to thank you for _____.

Responding to . . .

You're welcome.
Don't mention it.
No problem.
Glad to be of help.
It was nothing (at all).

I'm glad I could do it.
I'm glad I could help.
I'm glad I could be of help.
(It was) my pleasure.
Any time.

Appreciation

I appreciate it/that.
I'd appreciate it/that.
It's (very) nice/kind of you to offer.
Thanks for offering.
I appreciate your offering.
That's (very) nice/kind of you.
That would be nice.

You're very kind/nice.

I'm very grateful (to _____).

I really appreciate it.
I appreciate it very much.

It was very nice of you (to _____).

I can't begin to tell you how much I appreciate _____.

I want to express my appreciation to _____.

Persuading-Insisting

Listen!
Look!
(No,) really!
(No,) I mean it!
(No,) honestly!
(Oh,) come on!

I insist.

Let me, for a change.
Let me, for once.

There's no sense in your _____ing.
There's no reason (for you) to _____.
You don't have to _____.
You shouldn't have to _____.

Attracting Attention

Excuse me.

Initiating a Topic

You know, . . .

9

PERMISSION

Erica wants to take a photograph in the museum. What do you think she and the security guard are saying to each other?

Stuart Robinson is a guest at the Essex Hotel. He's asking the front desk manager for permission to do something. What do you think they're saying to each other?

park

A. Is parking **allowed**[1] here?
B. **Yes, it is.**[2]
A. Thanks.

take pictures

A. **Are you permitted to** take pictures[1] here?
B. **No, you aren't.**[3]
A. Oh, okay. Thanks.

surf

A. **Are people allowed to** surf[1] here?
B. **Yes, they are.**[2]
A. Thanks.

smoke

A. **Do they permit** smoking[1] here?
B. **I don't think so.**[3]
A. Oh, okay. Thanks.

[1] Is _____ing allowed/permitted?	[2] Yes, it is.	[3] No, it isn't.
Is it okay to _____?	Yes, it is.	No, it isn't.
Are you allowed/permitted to _____?	Yes, you are.	No, you aren't.
Are people allowed to _____?	Yes, they are.	No, they aren't.
Do they allow/permit _____ing?	Yes, they do.	No, they don't.
Do they allow people to _____?	Yes, they do.	No, they don't.
	[less certain]	[less certain]
	I think so.	I don't think so.
	I believe so.	I don't believe so.
	Yes, as far as I know.	Not as far as I know.

1. swim

2. camp

3. ice skate

4. skateboard

5. dive

6. picnic

7. play a radio

8. play frisbee

9. feed the animals

Ask somebody if you're allowed to do something.

Listening: *The Best Response*

Listen and choose the best response.

1. a. No, they aren't.
   b. Yes, they are.
   c. Yes, it is. (circled)

2. a. Yes, they are.
   b. No, you aren't.
   c. Yes, it is.

3. a. No, you aren't.
   b. No, you can't.
   c. No, it isn't.

4. a. Yes, as far as I know.
   b. No, it isn't.
   c. Yes, they do.

5. a. No, you aren't.
   b. No, they aren't.
   c. No, they don't.

6. a. I don't believe it.
   b. No, I don't think so.
   c. No, they don't.

7. a. No, they don't.
   b. Yes, you are.
   c. Yes, it is.

8. a. No, they don't.
   b. I don't think.
   c. No, it isn't.

9. a. I believe so.
   b. No, it isn't.
   c. Yes, they are.

10. a. Yes, they do.
    b. Yes, it is.
    c. Yes, as far as I know.

11. a. No, they aren't.
    b. No, it isn't.
    c. No, they don't.

12. a. No, you aren't.
    b. No, it isn't.
    c. No, they can't.

Grammar Check: *Gerunds and Infinitives*

1. Is _____ permitted here?
   a. to walk your dog
   b. walking your dog (circled)
   c. people

2. Do they allow _____ in the pool after midnight?
   a. people swimming
   b. to swim
   c. swimming

3. Are people permitted _____ on the test booklet?
   a. writing
   b. to write
   c. for writing

4. Is it okay _____ in this part of the woods?
   a. cutting down trees
   b. to cut down trees
   c. for people cutting down trees

5. As far as you know, are _____ permitted at the tennis club?
   a. bringing guests
   b. guests
   c. to bring guests

6. Do you think _____ is allowed in this pond?
   a. people fishing
   b. to fish
   c. fishing

7. _____ isn't permitted in this area of the park. Sorry.
   a. Picnic
   b. Picnicking
   c. Have a picnic

8. Excuse me. They don't allow _____ here in the aquarium.
   a. feed the fish
   b. people to feed the fish
   c. to feed the fish

Rules and Regulations

Working in small groups, think of all the rules and regulations you know—at school, at work, and in public places. Compare your list with the rules and regulations of other groups and compile a master list for everyone to look at. Then discuss with the class:

Do you agree or disagree with these rules?
Are there enough rules?
Are there too many rules?
What changes in rules and regulations would you make if you could?

InterAct!

New Rules and Regulations!

Decide on a place: a store, a museum, a public street, a beach, a park, a bus . . . any place you wish! Decide what the rules and regulations of that place are. Have other students *enter* your place and ask what *is* and *isn't* allowed there. Respond based on the rules you've created!

In Your Own Words

For Writing and Discussion

In the United States, some cities and towns allow retail stores to be open on Sundays. Others feel that there should be one day each week when shopping isn't allowed. What's your opinion? Can you think of reasons why stores should be permitted to open on Sundays? Can you also think of reasons why stores shouldn't be permitted to open? What about in your country? Are there similar rules and regulations?

A. **Excuse me**, [1] but **I don't think** picking the flowers **is allowed.**[2]
B. Oh?
A. Yes. There's a sign here that says so.
B. Hmm. "Please Don't Pick the Flowers." **Well, how about that!**[3]
   I guess I never noticed the sign. Thanks for telling me.
A. You're welcome.

[1] Excuse me,
    Pardon me,

[2] I don't think _____ing
    is allowed/permitted.
    I don't think you're
    allowed/permitted to
    _____.
    I don't think people are
    allowed/permitted to
    _____.
    I don't think they allow/
    permit people to
    _____.
    I don't think they allow/
    permit you to _____.

[3] (Well,) how about that!
    (Well,) what do you
    know!
    (Well,) how do you like
    that!
    (Well,) isn't that
    something!

1.

2.

3.

4.

5.

Tell somebody that something is not permitted.

150

Function Check: *What's My Line?*

Choose the appropriate line for Speaker A.

	A	**B**
1.	a. Excuse me. You're surfing. ⓑ Pardon me, but I don't think surfing is allowed here. c. Excuse me, but is surfing allowed here?	Oh. Thanks for telling me.
2.	a. Do you like that! Mondays! b. How do you like that! c. Is that something!	I know. I'm surprised, too. I can't believe the store is closed on Mondays.
3.	a. Is bringing floats into the water allowed here? b. Are floats allowed in the water here? c. Excuse me, but do they allow people to bring floats into the water here?	Yes, they do.
4.	a. Do you think sledding is permitted on the golf course? b. Well, what do you know! c. Isn't that something! No sledding!	I don't think so.
5.	a. Yes, it is. b. Is parking allowed here? c. There's a sign that says NO PARKING.	Well, isn't that something!
6.	a. Well, how do you like that! b. Excuse me, but do you think you're allowed to bring pets into the dorm? c. Pardon me, but pets aren't allowed in the dorm.	Not as far as I know.

InterChange

Look for at least ten signs in public places that tell what *is* and *isn't* allowed there. Write down what the sign says and compile a master list of signs that everyone in the class has found.

Be inventive! Create some new signs and create role plays with others in the class based on your signs.

have the car tonight

A. Could I ask you a favor?
B. Sure. What?
A. **Can I possibly**[1] have the car tonight?
B. Hmm. **Let me think for a minute.**[2] Well, **I guess so.**[3]
A. Thanks.

[1]
Can I (possibly) _____?
Could I (possibly) _____?
Can I please _____?
Could I please _____?
May I (please) _____?
Would it be possible for me to _____?
Is it all right/okay (with you) if I _____?
I'd like to _____, if that's all right/okay (with you).

[2]
Let me think (for a minute).
Let me see.
Let's see now.

[3]
I guess so.
I suppose so.
I don't see (any reason) why not.

1. go home an hour early today

2. stay over at Lucy's house tonight

3. borrow your computer until tomorrow

4. stay in my room a few hours past check-out time

5. put a hot tub on my balcony

Ask for permission to do something.

Function Check: *What's the Expression?*

1. _____ I ask you a favor?
   a. Maybe
   b. Would
   c. Could

2. Let me _____.
   a. see for a minute
   b. guess so
   c. think

3. Well, I _____.
   a. suppose now
   b. don't have any mind
   c. don't see why not

4. _____ it be possible for me to pick you up a little later?
   a. Would
   b. Could
   c. May

5. I'd like to pay for dinner, if _____.
   a. that's all right with you
   b. you suppose so
   c. you don't see any reason why not

6. _____ I please take a break now?
   a. Should
   b. Would
   c. May

7. _____ you possibly put money in the parking meter for me?
   a. Can
   b. Maybe
   c. Will

8. _____ leave now, if that's okay.
   a. It's all right to
   b. You can possibly
   c. I'd like to

9.
   Is it _____ if I dance with your wife?
   a. possible
   b. okay with you
   c. possibly

InterAct!

A Different Ending

Suppose the people on the previous page had responded differently!

Role play these new situations and present your *solutions* to the class.

serve leftovers for dinner?

Would you mind . . . ?

A. **Would you mind if I** served leftovers for dinner?(1)
B. No. **I wouldn't mind.**(2)
A. Are you sure? If you'd rather I didn't, I won't.
B. **No, honestly.**(3) If you want to serve leftovers for dinner, it's **all right**(4) with me. **Go right ahead.**(5)

turn up the heat?

Is it all right with you . . . ?

A. **Is it all right with you if I** turn up the heat?(1)
B. **Certainly.**(2)
A. Are you sure? If you'd rather I didn't, I won't.
B. **No, really.**(3) If you want to turn up the heat, it's **fine**(4) with me. **Be my guest.**(5)

(1) Would you mind if I _____ed?
     Would you object if I _____ed?
     Would it bother you if I _____ed?
     Do you mind if I _____?

⟶

(2) I wouldn't mind.
     I don't mind.
     It's all right with me.
     It's fine with me.
     It's okay with me.

Is it all right/okay (with you) if I _____?
Would it be all right/okay (with you) if I _____ed? ⟶
I'd like to _____, if that's all right/okay (with you).

Certainly.
Sure.
Of course.
By all means.
It's all right with me.
It's fine with me.
It's okay with me.

(3) No, honestly.
     No, really.

(4) all right
     fine
     okay

(5) Go (right) ahead.
     Be my guest.

1. Would you mind . . . ?

2. Is it all right with you . . . ?

3. Would it bother you . . . ?

4. I'd like to . . .

5. Do you mind . . . ?

6. Would you object . . . ?

7. Would it be all right with you . . . ?

8. Is it okay with you . . . ?

9. Would it bother you . . . ?

Give somebody permission to do something.

155

Function Check: *What's the Expression?*

1. _____ I drank the rest of your orange juice?
   a. Would you be all right if
   b. Do you bother
   c. Would it bother you if *(circled)*

2. No, _____ if you stayed at Peter's house tonight.
   a. it's all right
   b. of course
   c. I wouldn't mind

3. _____. If you want to buy new skates, it's fine with me.
   a. All means.
   b. Certainly.
   c. Don't let me stop.

4. _____ if we play one more set of tennis before we leave?
   a. Is it all right
   b. Would you like
   c. Are you okay

5. _____ okay with you if I stored my books in your attic?
   a. Certainly
   b. Would it be
   c. Would you be

6. _____ be all right if I kissed the groom?
   a. Will you
   b. Would it
   c. Do you

7. _____ to invite Patty to join us next Sunday.
   a. I'd like
   b. Would you mind
   c. Would you be bothered

8. _____. Ask Sarah for the car if you want to borrow it.
   a. It's sure with me.
   b. Go right with me.
   c. By all means.

9. *No. I don't mind if you rearrange all the furniture. _____.*
   a. You don't bother me.
   b. Be my guest.
   c. Go right.

Listening: *Who's Talking?*

Listen and decide what the relationship between the two speakers is.

1. a. roommate–roommate *(circled)*
   b. student–librarian
   c. surgeon–assistant

2. a. sports fan–baseball player
   b. photographer–actor
   c. citizen–police officer

3. a. waitress–chef
   b. mother–son
   c. cashier–customer

4. a. driver–passenger
   b. car salesman–customer
   c. diver–swimming coach

5. a. doctor–patient's wife
   b. husband–wife
   c. teacher–student

6. a. astronaut–astronaut
   b. teacher–student
   c. bride–groom

7. a. tenant–landlord
   b. customer–pet store owner
   c. zookeeper–visitor

8. a. guest–hotel manager
   b. student–student
   c. student–teacher

What's Your Opinion?

What's your opinion of the following situations on pages 154 and 155?

This father is about to prepare dinner. Do men and women share cooking responsibilities in your country? Also, what do you think about serving *leftovers*? Is this a common thing to do in your country? What leftovers might people serve?

This person is asking if he can come late to a party. If, for example, the party begins at 8:00 P.M., what time do you think is appropriate for him to arrive? Do you think he needs to let the person know he'll be late? Americans attach importance to being on time for events such as parties and meetings. Do you feel the same way?

InterAct!

Fickle People!

Some people are *fickle*—they just keep changing their minds!

Find a *fickle* partner. Choose a situation and create a role play in which one of you keeps making requests and then you change your mind. Present your role play to the class.

(1) Actually,
To be honest (with you),
To tell (you) the truth,

(2) I'd rather (that) you didn't.
I'd rather that you not.
I'd prefer it if you didn't.
I'd prefer that you not.
I'd prefer you not to.

(3) You see
The reason is

A. Would you mind if I ordered steak for two?
B. **Actually,**(1) **I'd rather you didn't.**(2)
A. Oh, okay.
B. **You see**(3) . . . I'm a vegetarian.
A. Oh, I'm sorry. I didn't know that.

1.

2.

3.

4.

5.

Function Check: *What's My Line?*

Choose the appropriate line for Speaker A.

	A	**B**
1.	a. Are you going to leave now? b. The reason is it's late. c. Do you mind if I leave now?	I'd rather you didn't.
2.	a. Actually, I'd prefer. b. I'd rather that you not. c. Would you mind if I didn't?	Okay. I won't.
3.	a. Would you object if you ate now? b. Actually, I didn't know that. c. Would it bother you if I ate now?	I'd prefer you not to.
4.	a. I'm allergic to strawberries. b. I'd prefer it if you didn't. c. To be honest with you.	I didn't know that.
5.	a. Oh, really? I didn't know that. b. You see, you're a vegetarian. c. Would it be okay if I served meat?	Actually, I'm a vegetarian.

(1. c. circled)

Listening: *Positive or Negative?*

Listen and decide whether the second speaker's response is positive or negative.

1. a. positive
    b. negative *(circled)*
	5. a. positive
	    b. negative
		9. a. positive
		    b. negative

2. a. positive
    b. negative
	6. a. positive
	    b. negative
		10. a. positive
		    b. negative

3. a. positive
    b. negative
	7. a. positive
	    b. negative
		11. a. positive
		    b. negative

4. a. positive
    b. negative
	8. a. positive
	    b. negative
		12. a. positive
		    b. negative

InterView

Working with a partner, think of a request to ask people in your class, in your school, where you work, or where you live. How many people respond positively to your request? How many respond negatively? Compare results with other students in the class.

the landlord
Mrs. Cramer

change the lock on our door

(1) authorization
permission
approval
consent
agreement

(2) authorize me to _____
permit me to _____
approve my _____ing
consent to my _____ing
agree to my _____ing

(3) make things difficult
    for you
make things complicated
    for you
complicate things
give you a hard time
give you "the runaround"

A. Could I ask you to change the lock on our door?
B. I'm afraid I can't do that without the landlord's **authorization**.[1]
A. Oh? How can I get her **authorization**?[1]
B. Just write a note to Mrs. Cramer and ask her to **authorize me to**[2] change the lock on your door.
A. Okay. I'll do that.
B. I don't mean to **make things difficult for you**.[3]
A. I understand.

the office manager
Mr. Fleming

1. fix the ceiling in my office

the payroll supervisor
Ms. Thompson

2. give me an advance on my next paycheck

your guidance counselor
Mr. Chen

3. switch my first and second period classes

the branch manager
Mrs. Watkins

4. leave our mail with our neighbors while we're away

the president
Ms. Blackwell

5. change my title to "Executive Director"

IMPORTANT MESSAGE
TO
WHILE YOU WERE OUT

Talk with somebody about how to get authorization to do something.

Function Check: *What's the Expression?*

1. I'm afraid I can't install a new telephone jack without _____ of my manager.
   a. permission
   b. the approval ✓
   c. agreement

2. Dr. Phillips, could you please _____ to enter the restricted ward of the hospital?
   a. approve me
   b. agree me
   c. authorize me

3. Did I make an adding mistake? I'm sorry, Mrs. Jones. I didn't mean to _____ for you.
   a. make things complicated
   b. give you a hard time
   c. runaround

4. At Blackwell State Prison, we don't _____ leave the grounds without permission.
   a. suppose anyone
   b. permit anyone to
   c. allow to

5. Guess what! Professor Thompson _____ doing research with her this summer.
   a. agreed my
   b. consented to my
   c. permitted me to

6. My kitchen sink is leaking very badly. Could I _____ fix it as soon as possible, Mr. Miller?
   a. ask you a favor
   b. agree to my
   c. ask you to

7.

   I'm sorry. I don't mean to _____ for you. But you need authorization to do that.
   a. *complicate*
   b. *make things difficult*
   c. *give you a hard time*

Personal Experiences

Talk with a partner about all the things you can think of that involve getting someone's authorization or permission. They may be at your school, at your job, where you live, or elsewhere.

Tell about experiences YOU have had when you needed to get somebody's authorization to do something. Was it easy to do, or did you get *the runaround*?

Compare stories with other students in the class and discuss when getting permission is necessary and when it just makes life difficult for people!

A landlord and a new tenant are talking about rules of the building. Practice this scene with a partner.

A. Before you sign the lease, do you have any questions?
B. Yes. Are we allowed to sublet the apartment?
A. No. I'm afraid subletting the apartment isn't permitted.
B. I see. Well, is it all right to use the fireplace?
A. No. You mustn't use the fireplace under any circumstances.
B. Oh. Well, do you allow people to have pets?
A. No. That's out of the question. We don't permit anyone to have pets.
B. How about parking in front of the building?
A. I'm sorry. You're not supposed to park in front of the building.
B. Oh.
A. And before I forget, I should mention that you may not alter the apartment in any way without permission. Now, do you have any other questions?
B. No, I guess not. I think you've answered them all.

A. Before _____, do you have any questions?
B. Yes. Are we allowed to _____?
A. No. I'm afraid _____ing isn't permitted.
B. I see. Well, is it all right to _____?
A. No. You mustn't _____ under any circumstances.
B. Oh. Well, do you allow people to _____?
A. No. That's out of the question. We don't permit anyone to _____.
B. How about _____ing?
A. I'm sorry. You're not supposed to _____.
B. Oh.
A. And before I forget, I should mention that you may not _____ without permission. Now, do you have any other questions?
B. No, I guess not. I think you've answered them all.

Now create original scenes with one or more partners based on the situations below. You can use the model on page 162 as a guide, but feel free to adapt and expand it any way you wish.

1. Before you begin your freshman year here at Winchester College, . . .

2. Before beginning your summer here at Camp Salamander, . . .

3. Before you start your six weeks of basic training, . . .

4. Before your tour of the Republic of Grenomia gets underway, . . .

Function Review: *Chapters 7, 8, 9*

Choose the appropriate line for Speaker A.

	A	**B**
1.	a. Would you like me to help you? b. I thought I might start my own company. ⓒ. I want to thank you for taking care of my plants while I was away.	Don't mention it.
2.	a. Would you like to join me? b. Do you prefer to go to a movie? c. If you'd rather I didn't call you, I won't.	I'd prefer you not to.
3.	a. I really appreciate it. b. Can I help you do that? c. It's nice of you to offer.	If you don't mind.
4.	a. I'm thinking of opening a restaurant. b. I don't think people are allowed to sail here. c. Can I count on you to finish this report?	Absolutely!
5.	a. I won't let you down. b. May I please leave early tonight? c. I'd rather you didn't.	It's okay with me.
6.	a. Is barbecuing allowed on the beach? b. Could I ask you a favor? c. Allow me to pull out your chair.	Not as far as I know.
7.	a. I might take a cruise down the Nile. b. Can I help? c. Can I count on you to close the store?	Wow!
8.	a. Is it all right with you if I use the copying machine right now? b. Here. Let me give you a hand. c. Could you possibly watch my bags for a minute?	Oh, I don't want to trouble you.
9.	a. I'd like to go home early, if that's okay. b. I'll probably lose my job soon. Business hasn't been very good. c. Would it be possible for me to take a business trip to London next month?	That's too bad.

John Stanley, a typical American businessman, rode to work on the subway one ordinary morning. He got off at his station downtown and walked to his office building. At the entrance, a security guard was posted to check employee ID cards. John reached into his pocket, but his wallet wasn't there! He was sure he had taken it from the dresser that morning. Of course he had, because it contained his subway pass, which got him on the train. John checked his other pockets, but his wallet was nowhere to be found. Someone had stolen it on the subway! His day was ruined! He couldn't even get into his own office!

For most Americans, the contents of a wallet are essential for everyday life. The wallet usually contains a driver's license, ID cards from one's job or school, credit cards, banking cards, a Social Security card, a library card, sports club or professional organization cards, and business cards—not to mention money, checks, and other important items. Having a wallet stolen represents not only a loss of money but a loss of time— perhaps time off from work—to report the theft and replace these necessary cards. A person must go through a lot of red tape and bureaucracy before his or her life returns to normal.

To get into his office, John had to call his boss and ask her to come to the security desk to vouch for him. Once in the office, John had to make numerous telephone calls to cancel his credit and banking cards and personal checks. He was put on *hold*, disconnected, and told several times to call back later. It was a frustrating experience, but he didn't give up until he had canceled all the cards. He didn't want anyone else spending his hard-earned money!

During lunch hour, John went to the nearest police station to fill out a report of the theft. Then he went to the bank to take out some money. He couldn't use the automatic banking machine without a card, so John had to stand in line for quite a long time. At the teller's window, he didn't have any identification to show, but he did have a copy of the police report. The teller compared his signature on the report with that on his signature card in the bank files, and he was able to withdraw some money.

John took the rest of the day off to replace his picture IDs. He went to the company's Personnel Office, to the Registry of Motor Vehicles, and to the university where he was taking evening courses. He didn't have to wait very long for these cards, but he did have to pay a replacement fee.

Losing a wallet can certainly be a frustrating experience. It represents not only the loss of money but a temporary loss of identity in a society full of numbers, cards, and documents. Just as there is little we can do about a pickpocket on the subway, there is little we can do to cut through all the red tape and bureaucracy of modern times.

InterAct!

Work with a group of students to create a dramatization of John Stanley's experience. Present your drama to the class.

Here are the expressions you practiced in Chapter 9. Try to use as many as you can to expand your vocabulary and to add variety to your use of English.

Permission

Asking for . . .

Can I (possibly) _____?
Could I (possibly) _____?
Can I (please) _____?
Could I (please) _____?
May I (please) _____?
Would it be possible for me to _____?
Is it all right/okay (with you) if
    I _____?
I'd like to _____, if that's all right/okay
    (with you).

Would you mind if I _____ed?
Would you object if I _____ed?
Would it bother you if I _____ed?
Do you mind if I _____?

Is it all right/okay (with you) if
    I _____?
Would it be all right/okay (with you)
    if I _____ed?
I'd like to _____, if that's all right/
    okay (with you).

Granting . . .

Certainly.
Sure.
Of course.
By all means.

It's all right with me.
It's fine with me.
It's okay with me.

I wouldn't mind.
I don't mind.

Go (right) ahead.
Be my guest.

I guess so.
I suppose so.
I don't see (any reason) why not.

If you want to _____,
    it's $\begin{cases} \text{fine} \\ \text{all right} \\ \text{okay} \end{cases}$ with me.

Denying . . .

I'd rather (that) you didn't.
I'd rather that you not.
I'd prefer it if you didn't.
I'd prefer that you not.
I'd prefer you not to.

_____ing isn't allowed/permitted.
You mustn't _____ (under any
    circumstances).
We don't permit anyone to _____.
You're not supposed to _____.
You may not _____ (without
    permission).

That's out of the question.

I can't do that without _____'s
    $\begin{cases} \text{authorization.} \\ \text{permission.} \\ \text{approval.} \\ \text{consent.} \\ \text{agreement.} \end{cases}$

Inquiring about Permissibility

Is _____ing allowed/permitted?
Is it okay to _____?
Is it all right to _____?
Are you allowed/permitted to _____?
Are people allowed to _____?
Do they allow/permit _____ing?
Do they allow people to _____?

Indicating Permissibility

I don't think _____ing is allowed/
    permitted.
I don't think you're allowed/permitted
    to _____.
I don't think people are allowed/
    permitted to _____.
I don't think they allow/permit people
    to _____.
I don't think they allow/permit you
    to _____.

Yes, _____ _____.
[less certain]
I think so.
I believe so.
Yes, as far as I know.

No, _____ _____.
[less certain]
I don't think so.
I don't believe so.
Not as far as I know.

Gratitude

Expressing . . .

Thanks (for telling me).

Apologizing

(Oh,) I'm sorry.

I don't mean to
    $\begin{cases} \text{make things difficult for you.} \\ \text{make things complicated for you.} \\ \text{complicate things.} \\ \text{give you a hard time.} \\ \text{give you "the runaround."} \end{cases}$

Attracting Attention

Excuse me, . . .
Pardon me, . . .

Surprise–Disbelief

Oh?

(Well,) how about that!
(Well,) what do you know!
(Well,) how do you like that!
(Well,) isn't that something!

Persuading–Insisting

No, honestly.
No, really.

Denying/Admitting

Admitting

You see . . .
The reason is . . .

Requests

Direct, Polite

Could I ask you to _____?

Could I ask you a favor?

Hesitating

Hmm.

Let me think (for a minute).
Let me see.
Let's see now.

SCENES & IMPROVISATIONS

These scenes review the functions and conversation strategies in Chapters 7, 8, and 9. Who do you think these people are? What do you think they're talking about? With other students, improvise conversations based on these scenes and act them out.

1.

2.

3.

4.

5.

6.

7.

8.

CHAPTER 1

Pages 2–3: "I Don't Think We've Met"

- It is common to initiate a conversation by introducing oneself.
- "Hello" is both formal and informal. "Hi" is informal, and therefore a more common form of greeting. "How do you do?" is a formal greeting.
- The subject and verb are often omitted in conversation, as in "(It's) nice to meet you" and "(I'm) happy to meet you."
- Appropriate questions to ask when people meet for the first time often involve what the two speakers have in common. For example, in an English class: "Where are you from?"; at a clinic: "Who is your doctor?"
- "What do you do?" is a very common question when two people meet. Profession and personal identity are strongly linked.
- It is NOT appropriate for people meeting for the first time to ask about salary, age, marital status, or religion.
- Short answers to information questions are more common in conversation than full-sentence answers. For example, "Where are you from?" "Japan," as opposed to "I'm from Japan." ("What do you do?" requires a full answer: "I'm a dancer.")
- In the question "Tell me, where are you from?," *tell me* is a polite opener to the question that follows. This expression is commonly used to signal to the listener that a question is going to be asked.
- *Small talk* refers to the kind of casual remarks that people make to each other when they first meet or are in situations where long conversations on serious topics are not appropriate or possible.

Exercises

6: Major = the field or major course of study (such as History, Chemistry, Philosophy) chosen by college students.

11: Be due = be scheduled to give birth.

Page 6: "Let Me Introduce . . ."

- The greetings "How are you doing?", "How are things?" and "How's it going?" are informal. "How are you?" and "How have you been?" are used in both formal and informal situations.
- "Meet _____" and "This is _____" are lines of introduction that are used in very informal situations.
- Short answers such as "Fine" and "All right" are very common in both formal and informal situations.
- The exchange "How are you?" "Fine" has become almost a ritual. The speaker asking the question "How are you?" is not necessarily asking how the other person is feeling, but rather is extending a greeting. In response to this "greeting," the other speaker automatically answers "Fine" or "Good," even if he or she isn't!

Page 7: "Don't I Know You From Somewhere?"

- "Excuse me, but . . ." is a common way to initiate a conversation. In this case, it is said with hesitation because Speaker A is not absolutely sure who Speaker B is.
- When a speaker uses a negative question to get information, the speaker expects a positive answer.

- The question "Don't I know you from somewhere?" is so common that it has become a type of cliché. It is sometimes used to indicate that the speaker has an ulterior motive (usually in striking up a conversation with a member of the opposite sex).
- In line 3, Speaker A is positive that he is correct and persists by saying "Sure" or "Of course."
- In line 4, Speaker B realizes that Speaker A has made a mistake. "No, I'm afraid not" and "You must have me confused with somebody else" are very polite ways of telling Speaker A that he is wrong.

Exercises

2: Boys and girls often play on the same team in certain sports such as baseball and tennis.

5: The FBI (Federal Bureau of Investigation) is the U.S. government agency that investigates federal crimes. The "10 Most Wanted" list is a constantly updated list of the most dangerous and sought-after criminals in the country.

Pages 10–11: "Guess Who I Saw Yesterday!"

- To say "Guess . . ." and "You won't believe . . ." are powerful ways to initiate a new topic of conversation and to capture the interest of the listener. These phrases signal to the listener that the topic and related information will be interesting and relevant.
- In line 5, the phrase "Sure you do!" emphasizes that Speaker A is VERY sure that Speaker B knows the person being talked about.
- In line 8, by saying "How IS she?" Speaker B is enthusiastically asking for information about the person mentioned.

Exercises

5: "Board of Education." Each city in the United States has a board or committee that makes major decisions concerning schools in the area.

6: Have a crush on = be infatuated with a member of the opposite sex.

7: "Retirement." When many older Americans stop working, usually around the age of 65, they often move to a warmer climate to spend their retirement years.

CHAPTER 2

Page 16: "Good News!"

- "I have some good news" is a common way to get someone's attention and set the scene for a happy announcement.
- In line 2, Speaker B is expressing interest in Speaker A's good news by saying "Really?"
- In lines 4 and 6, Speaker B appropriately reacts to Speaker A's good news by congratulating her friend.

Exercises

1–5: It is common to share with a friend one's good fortune (a new job, a promotion, acceptance to a university).

1: A raise = a raise in pay or salary.

2: Oxford University is a prestigious British university. For an American to be accepted by Oxford is a great honor.

3: Nobel Prizes are awarded annually to people who work for the interests of humanity. Examples are the Nobel Peace Prize, the Nobel Prize for Medicine, and the Nobel Prize for Literature.

4: Many companies give awards and recognition to hardworking employees as an incentive.

Page 17: "Bad News!"

• "I have some bad news" prepares the listener for an unpleasant announcement. The listener hears this and is prepared to sympathize.

Exercises

1: In the United States, dogs and cats are usually considered members of the family. For most Americans, losing a pet is a very serious matter.

Pages 20–21: "Have You Heard from . . . ?"

• To "hear from" and "be in touch with" can mean by letter or by telephone. To "talk to" and "speak to" can mean by telephone or face to face. To "run into" and "see" mean to meet someone face to face.

• In line 3, Speaker B says "As a matter of fact, I have" because it is a coincidence that Speaker A has mentioned that person.

• Even though the subject of the conversation is not present, it is appropriate to express congratulations or sympathy about what has been reported.

Exercises

6: The PTA (Parent Teacher Association) is a group of parents whose children attend the same school and who often meet with the school's teachers and other parents to discuss school issues and organize fundraising, social, and educational events for the school community.

Page 24: "What Do They Look Like?"

• In line 5, Speaker B says, "I'm afraid I don't remember what he looks like" as a polite way of asking Speaker A to describe the person.

• In line 7, Speaker A uses the expression "You can't miss him," meaning that Charlie Jones is VERY recognizable.

• When describing someone, the adjectives "heavy" and "thin" are more appropriate and polite than the adjectives "fat" and "skinny," which can be insulting.

Exercises

3: *Ms.* is a title for women that is commonly used in place of both Miss and Mrs.

Page 25: "What Are They Like?"

• In the expressions "They say . . ." and "They tell me . . . ," the pronoun "they" is used to mean "everybody" or "many people."

• In line 5, the phrase "Really? That's interesting" has very little meaning. It is most often used simply to acknowledge that the new information has been heard and understood.

Exercises

4: A senator is a U.S. political representative. Two senators from each of the fifty states are elected to represent their state in the United States Senate in Washington, D.C.

Pages 28–29: "Tell Me a Little About Yourself"

• In the first line, "So" signals a change in the topic of conversation.

• "Gee—uh . . ." and "Well, let's see . . ." are common ways to hesitate and give oneself time to think before speaking.

• "Tell me a little about yourself" is a very open-ended request. It is a common way of asking for information about a person being met for the first time.

• "What do you do?" (line 4) is probably the most common question asked when meeting someone for the first time. Americans generally define themselves and others by profession.

Exercises

2: The majority of American politicians pay writers to write their speeches for them.

A congresswoman or congressman is a political representative who serves in the U.S. House of Representatives in Washington, D.C.

4: Exercise classes, along with health food and jogging, have become more and more popular for both men and women in the United States.

CHAPTER 3

Page 34: "Which One?"

• In line 4, "Hmm" indicates that the speaker is thinking and trying to remember.

• In line 5, Speaker A says, "Don't you remember?" Speaker A is positive that Speaker B knows the object being talked about.

Page 36: "What's It Like There?"

• With the expressions "In my opinion . . . ," "If you ask me . . . ," and "As far as I'm concerned . . . ," a speaker focuses attention on the information to follow. These introductory phrases tell the listener that what follows is the speaker's opinion.

Page 38: "As Far as I Know . . ."

• "Do you/Would you by any chance know _____?" are polite ways of asking for information when approaching strangers.

• In line 3, Speaker B begins her answer to Speaker A's question by saying "As far as I know." This phrase is a common way to answer a question without appearing "too knowledgeable" and is therefore polite. Again in line 6, Speaker B is being polite when she says with uncertainty, "I don't think so." It isn't until Speaker A questions her certainty that Speaker B finally says, "Yes, I'm positive."

• In line 4, "Hmm" indicates that Speaker A is thinking about or "digesting" this new information.

• This lesson illustrates the importance of the notion of time and schedule to Americans. In the model conversation, Speaker A is extremely concerned about the arrival time of the president. In the exercises, similar concern about time is expressed.

Page 40: "Did You Remember?"

• "Uh-oh!" is a common expression used when someone suspects that something bad has happened.

• A family dog is considered important enough in the United States that if it is not fed on schedule, there is concern.

• In line 4, "Well," signals that the speaker has accepted the situation and is ready to decide on what action is to be taken.

- In lines 4 and 5, "I guess one of us should go and do it" is similar to a suggestion. Speaker B is really suggesting that Speaker A do what was forgotten, but does not say so directly.

Exercises
2: It is becoming more common for husbands and wives to share household chores such as cleaning, cooking, and setting the table.

Page 42: "Did You Hear?"

- The announcement on the radio that schools are closed is probably due to a snowstorm. This is common during winter storms when traveling to school could be dangerous.

Exercises
4: City Hall is the location of the offices of city government.

Page 43: "Have You Heard the News?"

- Declarative sentences spoken with question intonation are common ways of expressing surprise and disbelief. ("They're going to make the park across the street into a parking lot?!")

Pages 46–47: Communicators

- It is common and often considered polite to encourage a person telling a story by asking questions as the events unfold: "And then what did you do?" "What did you do after that?" This shows interest on the part of the listener.

CHAPTER 4

Page 54: "What Did You Say?"

- In line 2, Speaker B says, "I'm sorry." It is polite to apologize when asking for repetition. It is less polite simply to say "What?" or "Huh?"

Page 56: "I'm Sorry. I Didn't Hear You"

- By emphasizing the question word "WHEN. . .?" or "WHAT . . .?", Speaker B is indicating which piece of information he failed to hear or is not sure he heard correctly.

Pages 58–59: "Have You Got It?"

- When asking strangers, the polite forms "Could you please tell me _____?," "Could you possibly tell me _____?," and the like are more appropriate than direct questions such as "How do you get to the post office?"
- The expressions "Have you got it?," "Got it?," "Have you got that?," "Got that?," "Do you follow me?," "Okay?," and "Do you think you've got it now?" are used to check whether the person you are talking to has understood what you have said.
- The expressions "Let me see," "Let me see if I understand," and "Let me see if I've got that right" are used to check your own understanding of what someone else has said. They would normally be followed by a repetition of the information that you are checking.
- The expressions "Uh-húh," "Um-hḿm," "Yes," "That's right," and "Right" are used to show that what the other speaker has said is correct. They give encouragement and tell the speaker to continue talking.
- In line 8, "Hmm . . ." indicates that the speaker has momentarily forgotten and is thinking.
- In line 10, by saying "Okay" the speaker indicates that she has understood.

Exercises
2: Self-service gas stations are popular. If gas customers pump their own gas, they usually pay less money for it.

Pages 62–63: Communicators

- The expressions "Are you with me (so far?)," "Okay (so far)?," "Are you following me (so far)?" and "Have you got all that?" are used to check another person's understanding of what you have said.
- The expressions "I'm following you," "I've got it," "I understand," "I see," and "I'm with you" indicate that you have understood what the other person has said.

CHAPTER 5

Page 68: "Thanks for Saying So"

- In line 2, Speaker B asks, "Did you really like it?" This is a polite and gracious way to respond to a compliment. It indicates that the speaker is pleased, yet humble.
- Expressing gratitude is expected when responding to a compliment: "Thanks/Thank you (for saying so)," or "It's nice of you to say so/that."

Page 69: "You're Just Saying That!"

- A typical way to make a compliment is by saying you like something and then telling why with a descriptive adjective. The superlative adjective is used to make a strong compliment.
- Instead of responding to a compliment with a simple "Thank you," the following exchange is very common. The speaker responds to a compliment with an expression of disbelief: "Oh, go on! You're just saying that!" The speaker is not questioning the other person's sincerity, but instead is responding to the compliment with humility. The other person then normally insists that the compliment was sincere: "No, I mean it!" "I'm (really) serious," or "I'm being honest with you."

Exercises
3: "Interesting" is an adjective with little meaning. The speaker is either not sure how she feels about the painting or, out of politeness, does not wish to say what she *really* thinks about it!

Page 72: "Just What I Had in Mind!"

- A declarative sentence with question intonation is often used to check whether the other speaker is satisfied. For example, line 3: "It isn't too heavy?", line 7: "So you're satisfied with it?"

Page 74; "I'd Like a Refund, Please"

- These expressions are used to find out the cause of a person's dissatisfaction: "What seems to be the problem (with it)?," "What seems to be the matter (with it)?," "What's the problem (with it)?," "What's the matter (with it)?," "What's wrong (with it)?"
- It is not unusual to return something you have purchased or you have received as a gift. Most department stores have a Return Counter. A store will usually give a refund (return your money) and/or allow you to exchange the item for another and pay any difference in cost. Some stores won't give refunds or exchanges. If they don't, there are usually signs in the store telling a customer the store policy.
- In line 5, the customer uses the polite expression "I don't think so" or any of the alternatives rather than simply saying "No."

- In lines 8 and 10, the customer expresses surprise and disappointment when she exclaims, "No refunds?" and "Oh."

Exercises

2: Flashy = very brightly colored, often with a wild pattern.

Page 76: "I Was a Little Disappointed"

- By beginning a response with "To tell (you) the truth,/Honestly,/To be honest (with you)," the speaker is setting the scene for expressing a reaction of disappointment about something.
- "I was (a little) disappointed," "I wasn't very pleased with it," and "It was a little disappointing" are expressions of disappointment and are also used as a way of complaining.

Page 78: "I'm Really Annoyed"

- To be "mad at," "angry at," and "furious with" are very strong emotional states.
- Voicing a complaint to a friend is different from and much easier than complaining directly to the person responsible for the annoyance.
- In line 6, Speaker B says, "I don't understand." Speaker B sees a direct and logical solution to the problem and cannot understand why Speaker A has not taken this step.
- The present continuous tense is often used to express a habitual action when emphasizing the frequency of the action.

Pages 80–81: Communicators

- The questions "Would you like to _____?" and "Do you want to _____?" are very similar.
- By saying "Well," before answers and questions, the speakers are being polite by avoiding being too direct.
- In line 26, Speaker A says, "But if you don't like seafood, we can go someplace else." He assumes that Speaker B will reject this suggestion since she has rejected every other one!
- After this long discussion, Speaker B says, "Then it's settled" or any of the alternative lines. This indicates that a good decision for both speakers has been made.

CHAPTER 6

Page 86: "I'd Prefer a Baked Potato"

- Restaurants almost always offer a choice of side dishes with the main course. In addition, a choice of dressings is offered (French, Italian, Russian, blue cheese).
- When ordering items on a menu, the indefinite article "a/an" is normally used. For example, "I'll have a hamburger, a salad . . ." When the particular food being ordered is a specialty of the restaurant, the definite article is used. For example, "I'll have the chicken, the fish . . ." In this case, the particular dish is listed as a specialty on the menu and the definite article refers to that specific dish.
- The amount of cooking time for beef (steak, hamburger, roast beef) varies from *rare* (the shortest cooking time), *medium rare*, *medium*, *medium well* to *well done* (the longest cooking time).

Page 88: "I'd Much Rather See a Movie"

- Accompanying a preference with expressions such as "To be honest" or "I think" and asking "Is that okay?" is

a polite way of showing that the speaker is being considerate of the other person's feelings.

Pages 90–91: "A Serious Disagreement"

- Line 1: "You've seemed troubled for the past few days" makes it clear that Speakers A and B are close enough friends that A has noticed a change in B's behavior. Since they are good friends, Speaker A feels that it is appropriate to ask questions about B's problem.
- In line 2, "Well, to tell the truth" indicates that Speaker B is about to admit that there is a problem.
- In line 4, Speaker B says "To make a long story short, ..." This expression is used when people want to leave out details and get right to the main point.

Exercises

5: Disney World is a popular family vacation spot in Orlando, Florida.

6: Older relatives are sometimes sent to special homes for senior citizens where they are taken care of by professional nurses, doctors, physical therapists, activity and recreation personnel, and other staff. Nursing homes vary widely in terms of the quality of staff and facilities.

7: A parish is a local church community.

9: Workers sometimes go on strike (stop working) if they have a serious disagreement with their employers.

Page 94: "It Doesn't Make Any Difference"

- In line 3, Speaker A asks, "You don't have any strong feelings about it?" Declarative sentences are often used as questions to check understanding.
- At large parties, especially at open house parties, guests do not necessarily arrive at the party or leave at specific times. Rather, they may arrive and leave as they wish.

Page 96: "It's Entirely Up to You"

- In line 3, Speaker A is being very considerate and respectful of Speaker B by double-checking "Are you sure?" and by using the expression "I mean . . ." along with the polite statement that follows.
- In line 4, Speaker B is being equally as polite and considerate by saying "Honestly" along with his statements of indifference.

Exercises

5: "Security blanket." Young children often choose a special blanket which they like to have with them at all times "for security." The child in Exercise 5 is about ten years old, and the mother feels that it is certainly time for her daughter to give up her security blanket.

Pages 98–99: Communicators

- The expressions: "Well, . . ." "Let me see, . . ." "Hmm, . . ." "Okay, . . ." "Uh, . . ." "I think, . . ." and "I guess, . . ." are common ways of hesitating or "buying time" until you think of what you want to say.

CHAPTER 7

Page 106: "I Promise"

- To say the words "I promise" is to make a strong commitment to do something.
- In line 3, Speaker A emphasizes the importance of his request by double-checking with Speaker B: "You won't forget? It's really important."

- In line 4, recognizing how important this request is to Speaker A, Speaker B reassures him by saying "Don't worry. You can rely on me."

Exercises
5: In order to operate, restaurant kitchens must maintain a standard of cleanliness determined by the local government. A health inspector makes periodic visits to check that these standards are followed.

Page 107: "I Won't Let You Down"

- In lines 3 and 5, Speaker A checks with Speaker B: "Can I depend on that?" "I'm counting on you." The request is clearly important enough for the speaker to ask for reassurance twice.
- The single word expressions "Absolutely!," "Definitely!," and "Positively!" indicate a strong statement of commitment.
- In line 5, Speaker A says "Okay" after Speaker B repeats his promise. This is a common way of responding to a promise and means "We both understand."
- A businessperson's workday normally begins at 9 A.M. and ends at 5 P.M. This businessman clearly needs his car by the end of the workday so that he can drive home.

Exercises
1: For a portion of the summer, children are often sent to overnight camp for fun and exercise (and to give their parents a vacation!).

Pages 110–111: "He Gave Me His Word"

- "How come?" is equivalent to "Why?"
- In line 7, the expression "After all" implies "It's logical."

Exercises
4: Workers are often paid time-and-a-half or double for overtime hours.

Page 114: "I've Made a Decision"

- The expression "You know" has a variety of meanings in English. In this instance, "You know" specifically introduces a new topic of conversation.
- "Gee!," "Boy!," and "Wow!" are informal expressions for indicating surprise.
- In line 4, Speaker B expresses surprise and also comments on the importance of what Speaker A has announced: "That's a big decision!"

Page 116: "I'll Probably Stay Home and Read a Book"

- The greeting "Hi! It's me!" is a casual way to begin a telephone conversation. The speakers clearly know each other well enough to recognize one another's voice.
- In line 2, Speaker B answers "Oh, hi!" In this case, "Oh," indicates that Speaker B understands who "me" is in line 1.
- In line 3, Speaker A begins his question with "Tell me, . . ." This expression indicates that Speaker A wants to get directly to the point, the reason that he is calling.
- In line 3, when Speaker A asks "what are you doing this afternoon?," an invitation will probably follow. By responding "I'm not sure. I'll probably . . ." and asking "How about you?," Speaker B is communicating the fact that he IS open to suggestions.
- In line 6, Speaker A says "Well," before announcing his plans. "Well," is used because the speaker wishes to avoid being too direct.

Page 118: "I Haven't Made Up My Mind Yet"

- In line 1, "to ask" means "to invite."
- A prom is a formal dance, usually for high school students (ages 14–18). The senior prom, a tradition in many high schools, is a dance attended by members of the senior class during their last year of high school.
- "Then again" is similar to "on the other hand" and indicates that the speaker will follow with another option.
- The subject "it" is sometimes dropped in casual conversation. In line 4, Speaker A says, "Sounds like a difficult decision" ("It sounds like a difficult decision.")
- Similarly, short questions such as "Promise?" ("Do you promise?") and short answers such as "Promise." ("I promise") are common in conversation.

Exercises
4: Break up with = end a romantic relationship with someone.

Page 120: "I Was Planning to Do Room 407 a Little Later"

- In line 1, to "do" a room means to clean it.
- In line 2, Speaker B makes an excuse to a superior by stating a past intention: "I was planning to do it a little later."

Pages 122–123: Communicators

- To say "Let's have lunch together sometime soon" is not necessarily an invitation. It is a common and polite way of saying good-bye.

CHAPTER 8

Page 128: "Do You Want Me to Wash the Dishes?"

- "No. Don't worry about it" and "That's okay/all right" are polite ways of declining an offer.
- When making an offer and then being refused, persuading or insisting is considered polite and very appropriate.
- When responding to an offer, appreciation, in addition to gratitude, is the expected response.

Page 129: "Want Any Help?"

- Making an observation ("I see you're changing the oil") is a common way to initiate a conversation.
- Dropping the auxiliary and subject from the beginning of questions is common in casual conversation. For example, "(Do you) want any help?"
- "If you don't mind," "If you wouldn't mind," and "If it's no trouble" are common and polite ways of accepting an offer.

Pages 132–133: "Let Me Give You a Hand"

- In line 6, Speaker A interrupts Speaker B as he is trying to refuse the offer. By doing this, along with strongly insisting and even ordering ("You're not moving that desk by yourself!"), Speaker A is not being rude. Rather, Speaker A is showing care and concern for Speaker B.

Page 136: "May I Help You?"

- "May I help you?" and "Can I help you?" are common expressions used by salespeople when approaching customers.

- In line 2, Speaker B responds to Speaker A's offer of help by saying "I'm just looking." This expression is commonly used when you don't want a salesperson's assistance.
- In line 5, Speaker A begins to tell Speaker B that the store doesn't have any digital watches by saying "I'm afraid . . ." This expression is a polite way of giving bad news.
- In line 8, "I guess not" is a polite way of saying "No" to the salesperson.

Exercises

5: More and more sugar-free food products are being produced, due to consumers' concern about their weight, the care of their teeth, and their general health.

Page 138: "Can I Do Anything to Help?"

- In line 2, Speaker B hesitates when responding to Speaker A ("Well, uh . . .") because he has just been hurt and is not sure how to answer.
- Rollerblading on city streets is a popular activity in many parts of the United States.
- In line 5, Speaker A reacts to Speaker B's accident by saying "Oh, no!" This indicates that he thinks the accident was a terrible thing and that he sympathizes with Speaker B.
- In line 7, Speaker A is offering his hand to help Speaker B up when he says "Well, here."
- When offering help, "Allow me . . ." is formal and very polite.

Exercises

1: To be mugged means to be attacked by a thief on the street.

Page 140: "I'm Very Grateful to You"

- In this conversation, Speaker A strongly insists on thanking Speaker B because the favor (lending the calculator) was an important one.

Exercises

5: Fix someone up = arrange for two people to meet each other with the hope that they will become romantically involved.

Page 142: Communicators

- At a formal award ceremony such as this, very formal and flowery language is appropriate and expected.

CHAPTER 9

Pages 146–147: "Is Parking Allowed Here?"

- The passive construction and the pronouns "they" and "you" are most often used when referring to some authority. The identity or source of this authority is not known or important. "They" can also refer to unnamed people in general. For example, "They say it's beautiful in Puerto Rico." "They say she's an excellent surgeon."
- In models 2 and 4, Speaker A says "Oh, okay" as a way of accepting the negative response he or she has just been given by Speaker B.

Page 150: "Please Don't Pick the Flowers"

- In line 1, Speaker A is trying to be polite and not seem critical of Speaker B's actions by using the less direct "Excuse me, but I don't think . . ."
- In line 4, "Hmm" indicates that Speaker B is considering this new information while reading the sign.

Page 152: "Can I Possibly Have the Car Tonight?"

- In line 1, before Speaker A directly asks for permission, he says "Could I ask you a favor?" He does this to signal to Speaker B that he wishes to make a request.
- Saying "Yes" tentatively can be done by using the expressions "I guess so," "I suppose so", and "I don't see (any reason) why not."

Exercises

5: A hot tub (pronounced "HOT tub") is a large tub filled with very warm water in which one or more people sit to relax. Hot tubs are very popular in the United States, especially on the West Coast.

Pages 154–155: "Would You Mind If I Served Leftovers for Dinner?"

Models

- Leftovers consist of food not eaten at a previous meal that is served at a later meal.
- In line 3 of the first model, "No" indicates a positive response to Speaker A's request for permission.

Exercises

2: To skip dessert means to go without it.

8: A teddy bear is a stuffed toy in the shape of a bear that is named after Theodore "Teddy" Roosevelt, the twenty-sixth president of the United States.

Page 158: "I'd Rather You Didn't"

- The expressions "You see," and "The reason is" are used to preface an admission.
- In line 3, "Oh," indicates that Speaker A was expecting a positive response to his request. He acknowledges the negative response when he says "okay."
- In line 5, "Oh," indicates that Speaker A understands Speaker B's reason for denying permission. Speaker A also politely apologizes for not knowing the reason beforehand.

Page 160: "I Can't Do That Without an Authorization"

- In line 2, Speaker B politely begins his negative response by saying "I'm afraid I can't . . ."
- In line 3, "Oh?" indicates that Speaker A is surprised and a little disappointed at the negative response.
- In this conversation, Speaker B apologizes for not having the authority himself to do what Speaker A wants. Speaker A's "I understand" indicates that she recognizes that another authority is responsible and not Speaker B.

Advice–Suggestions

Asking for . . .

Any suggestions?   5

Offering . . .

Why don't you _____?   5

How about _____ing? \
What about _____ing? \
Let's _____. \
Why don't we _____? \
We could _____. \
Would you be interested in \
     _____(ing)?   5

Maybe we should _____. \
Maybe we shouldn't _____.   5

They say that _____ is very good.   5 \
One of my favorite _____s is _____.   5

Is _____ okay?   5

Agreement/Disagreement

Expressing Agreement

I agree (with you). \
You're right. \
[less formal] \
I'll say! \
You can say that again!   7

Apologizing

I'm sorry. \
Excuse me.   1

(Oh,) I'm sorry.   9

I don't mean to
- make things difficult for you.
- make things complicated for you.
- complicate things.
- give you a hard time.
- give you "the runaround."   9

Appreciation

I appreciate it/that. \
I'd appreciate it/that. \
It's (very) nice/kind of you to offer. \
Thanks for offering. \
I appreciate your offering. \
That's (very) nice/kind of you. \
That would be nice.   8

I really appreciate it. \
I appreciate it very much.   8

It was very nice of you (to _____).   8

I want to express my appreciation \
     to _____.   8

I can't begin to tell you how much I \
     appreciate _____.   8

You're very kind/nice.   8

Asking for and Reporting Information

Where are you from? \
     Japan. \
What do you do? \
     I'm an *English teacher*. \
Which *apartment do you live in?* \
How long *have you been studying here?* \
Who *is your doctor?* \
Whose *family are you in?* \
What kind of *music do you play?* \
When *are you due?*   1

How about you? \
What about you? \
And you?   1

Have you
- heard from
- run into
- talked to
- seen
- spoken to
- been in
-    touch with

_____ lately?   2

How's _____ doing? \
How is _____? \
How has _____ been?   2 \
     Fine. \
     Great. \
     Wonderful. \
     Not too well. \
     Not so well. \
     Not very well.   2

Did _____ have anything to say?   1

Have you heard anything about _____? \
Do you know anything about _____?   2

Tell me a little about yourself.   2

What do you want to know? \
What would you like to know? \
What can I tell you?   2

Do you (by any chance) know _____? \
Do you happen to know _____? \
Would you happen to know _____?   3

Could you (please) tell me _____? \
Could you (possibly) tell me _____? \
Do you (by any chance) know _____? \
Would you (by any chance) \
     know _____? \
Can you (please) tell me _____? \
Would you (possibly) be able to tell me \
     _____? \
Would you by any chance be able to \
     tell me _____?   4

Did you hear that _____?   3

Where did you hear that? \
How do you know (that)? \
Who told you (that)?   3

*School isn't really going to be closed \
     tomorrow,* is it?   3

What happened?   3

Have you by any chance \
     ever _____ed?   3

Can you tell me what it's like?   3 \
Which one is that?   3

People say . . . \
They say . . . \
People tell me . . . \
Everybody says . . . \
Everybody tells me . . . \
I've heard . . . \
Word has it (that) . . .   2

I heard it on the radio/on TV/on the \
     news. \
I saw/read it in the paper.   3

Asking for and Reporting Additional Information

What else have you heard? \
Have you heard anything else? \
Do you know anything else?   2

Can you tell me anything else? \
Can you tell me anything more? \
What else can you tell me?   3

What did you do next? \
What did you do after that? \
And then what did you do? \
What was the next thing you did?   3

What else would you like to know?   3

As a matter of fact, . . . \
In fact, . . .   3

Asking for Repetition

(Sorry.) I didn't hear you.   4

I didn't (quite) catch that. \
I didn't get that. \
I missed that. \
I'm lost. \
I'm not following you.   4

What did you say? \
Could you (please) repeat that? \
Would you (please) repeat that? \
Could you say that again? \
Would you say that again? \
Would you mind saying that again? \
Would you mind repeating that?   4

WHEN do you want me to _____? \
WHEN should I _____? \
WHEN did you tell me to _____?   4

Could you repeat
- instructions?
- directions?
- steps?
- things you said?   4

the last two

I forgot the last part.   4

Attracting Attention

Excuse me, . . . \
Pardon me, . . .   8, 9

Certainty/Uncertainty

Inquiring about . . .

Are you positive/certain/sure
  (about that)?   3

Expressing Certainty

I'm positive/certain/sure.
I'm absolutely positive/certain/sure.
I'm a hundred percent sure.
There's no doubt about it.
I'm absolutely positive.   3

Expressing Uncertainty

I don't know for sure.
I'm not (completely) positive.
I'm not absolutely positive.
I'm not a hundred percent positive.   3

I'm not sure.
I'm not certain.
I don't know yet.   9

I don't think so.
Not as far as I know.   3

I doubt it.   3

Checking and Indicating Understanding

Checking Another Person's Understanding

Have you got it?
Got it?
Have you got that?
Got that?
Do you follow me?
Okay?   4

Are you with me (so far)?
Okay (so far)?
Are you following me (so far)?   4

Do you think you've got it now?
Have you got all that?   4

Checking One's Own Understanding

Let me see.
Let me see if I understand.
Let me see if I've got that.
Let me see if I've got that right.
Let me repeat that back.   4

Indicating Understanding

I'm following you.
I've got it.
I understand.
I see.
I'm with you.   4

Uh-húh.
Um-hḿm.
Yes.
That's right.
Right.   4

Complaining

It's too _____.   5

I was (a little) disappointed.
I wasn't very pleased with it.
It was (a little) disappointing.   5

I'm { annoyed with / upset with / [stronger] / mad at / angry at / furious with } _____.   5

He's always / He's constantly / He keeps on } _____ing.   5

His _____ing { bothers / annoys / upsets } me.   5

I'm tired of _____(ing).
I'm sick of _____(ing).
I sick and tired of _____(ing).   5

Complimenting

Expressing Compliments

That was { a very good / quite a / [less formal] / some } _____!   5

I thought it was { excellent. / wonderful. / terrific. / magnificent. / fabulous. / superb. }   5

I (really) like _____.
I love _____.   5

It's very _____.
It's so _____.   5

It's one of the _____est _____s I've
  ever _____ed.   5

Responding to Compliments

Thanks (for saying so).
Thank you (for saying so).
It's nice of you to say so.
It's nice of you to say that.
I'm glad you like it.   5

Oh/Aw, go on!
Oh/Aw, come on!
Oh!   5

You're just saying that!   5

Congratulating

That's fantastic!
That's great!
That's wonderful!
That's exciting!
That's marvelous!   2

Congratulations!   2

I'm very happy to hear that.
I'm very happy for you.   2

Deduction

You must be _____.   2

Denying/Admitting

Admitting

You see . . .
The reason is . . .   9

Describing

He's/She's about your height, sort of
  heavy, with *dark curly* hair.   2

He's/She's very _____.   2

It's the _____ one with the _____.   3

It's a very _____ _____.   3

It's one of the _____est _____s
  I know.   3

Directions–Location

Asking for Directions

Could you please tell me how to get
  to _____?   4

Giving Directions

Go to _____.
Turn _____.
Walk _____ blocks.   4

Disappointment

I was (a little) disappointed.
I wasn't very pleased with it.
It was (a little) disappointing.   5

I'm (very) disappointed with/
  in _____.   7

Focusing Attention

As a matter of fact, . .
In fact, . . .   3

If you ask me, . . .
In my opinion, . . .
As far as I'm concerned, . . .   3

What it boils down to is that . . .
The fact of the matter is that . . .
As it turned out, . . .   7

Gratitude

Expressing

Thanks (very much).
Thank you (very much).   8

Thanks (for telling me).   9

Thank you for *saying so*.
It's nice of you to *say that/so*.   5

I'm very grateful (to _____).   8

I want to thank _____.
I want to express my gratitude
  to _____.   8

I keep forgetting to thank you
  for _____.   8

Responding to . . .

You're welcome.
Don't mention it.
No problem.
Glad to be of help.
It was nothing (at all).   8

I'm glad I could do it.
I'm glad I could help.
I'm glad I could be of help.
(It was) my pleasure.
Any time.   8

Greeting People

Hello.
[less formal]
Hi.
[more formal]
How do you do?   1

(It's) nice to meet you.
(It's) nice meeting you.
(I'm) happy to meet you.
(I'm) glad to meet you.
(I'm) pleased to meet you.   1

How are you?
How have you been?
[less formal]
How are you doing?
How are things?
How's it going?
   Fine (thank you/thanks).
   Good.
   All right.
   Okay.
   Not bad.   1

Hesitating

Hmm.   6,9
Uh . . .   6
Gee-uh . . .   2
Well . . .   6
Let me see . . .
Let's see . . .
(Well,) let's see . . .
Let's see now . . .   2,6,9
Let me think (for a minute).   9
I think . . .
I guess . . .   6
I don't know where to begin.
I don't know where to start.
I don't know what to say.   2

Identifying

My friend *Paul*, my brother *Tom*, . . .   1
She's the one who _____.   1
The one *the children gave you*.   3

Indifference

Whenever _____ is fine with me.
(Whoever . . . Whatever . . . However . . .
   Whichever . . . Wherever . . .)   6
It doesn't make any difference (to me).
It doesn't matter (to me).
It's all the same to me.
I don't care.
I don't feel strongly about it one way or
   the other.   6
It doesn't matter to me whether you
   _____ or not.   6

It's (entirely) up to you.
It's (entirely) your decision.
It's for you to decide.   6

Initiating a Topic

You know, . . .   7,8
I have some good/bad news.   2
Have you heard the news?   3
Guess _____!
You won't believe _____!   8
Tell me, . . .   1

Initiating Conversations

Excuse me, but . . .
Pardon me, but . . .   1
I don't think we've met.   1
Don't I know you from somewhere?   1
Hi! It's me!   7
Well, if it isn't _____!   7

Instructing

(Please) _____.
First, . . .
Then, . . .
After that, . . .
Next, . . .
And finally, . . .   4

Intention

Inquiring about . . .

What are you doing *this afternoon?*   7
Have you decided _____?   7

Expressing . . .

I'm going to _____.
I'm planning to _____.
I plan to _____.
I intend to _____.
I've decided to _____.   7
I've been thinking of _____ing.
I'm thinking of _____ing.
I've been thinking about _____ing.
I'm thinking about _____ing.   7
I've been meaning to _____ (for a
   long time).   7
I've thought about it for a long time.
I've given it a lot of thought.
I've given it a lot of serious
   consideration.   7
I've decided it's time to do it.   7
I haven't made up my mind yet.   7
I was planning to _____.
I was going to _____.
I intended to _____.
I thought I would _____.   7
I was intent on _____ing.
I was determined to _____.   7

I'll _____ { right away.
       right now.
       as soon as I can.
       the first chance I get.   7

Introductions

Introducing Oneself

My name is _____.
I'm _____.   1

Introducing Others

Let me introduce (you to) _____.
I'd like to introduce (you to) _____.
I'd like you to meet _____.
[less formal]
Meet _____.
This is _____.   1

Invitations

Extending . . .

Would you like to join me?
Do you want to join me?
Would you be interested in
   joining me?   7

Accepting . . .

I'd love to.
I'd like to.
I'd like that.   7

Likes/Dislikes

Inquiring about . . .

How do you like _____?
What do you think of _____?   5
How did you like _____?   5
Did you like _____?   5
Don't you like _____?   5

Expressing Likes

I like _____.
I love _____.   5

Expressing Dislikes

I don't like _____ very much.
I don't enjoy _____ very much.
I don't (particularly) care for _____.
I'm not (really) crazy about _____.
[stronger]
I hate _____.   5

Offering to Do Something

Do you want me to _____?
Would you like me to _____?
I'll _____, if you'd like.
I'll be happy/glad to _____, if
   you'd like.
I'd be happy/glad to _____, if
   you'd like.   8
Let me (_____).   8

Offering to Help

Making an Offer

(Do you) want any help?
(Do you) need any help?
(Do you) want a hand?
(Do you) need a hand?
Can I help?
Can I give you a hand?　　　　　　　8

Would you like me to help you _____?
Do you want me to help you _____?
I'd be glad/happy to help you _____,
　　(if you'd like).
Let me help you _____.
Would you like any help _____ing?
Would you like me to give you a hand
　　_____ing?　　　　　　　　　　8

Can I do anything to help?
Is there anything I can do to help?
Can I help?　　　　　　　　　　　8

I'd be happy/glad to give you a hand.
I'd be happy/glad to lend a hand.
I'd be happy/glad to help.　　　　　8

Let me give you a hand.
I'm happy to lend a hand.　　　　　8

Let me _____.
Allow me to _____.　　　　　　　8

May I help you?
Can I help you?　　　　　　　　　8

Is there anything/something in
　　particular I can help you find?
Is there anything/something you're
　　looking for in particular?　　　8

Is there anything else I can help
　　you with?　　　　　　　　　　8

Please let me know if I can be of any
　　further assistance.
Please feel free to call on me if I can be
　　of any further assistance.
If I can be of any further assistance,
　　please don't hesitate to ask/let
　　me know.　　　　　　　　　　8

Responding to an Offer

If you don't mind.
If you wouldn't mind.
If it's no trouble.　　　　　　　　8

I don't
want to
{
trouble you.
bother you.
inconvenience you.
put you to any trouble.
put you out.　　　　　　　　　　8
}

Don't worry about it.
That's okay/all right.　　　　　　8

Permission

Asking for . . .

Can I (possibly) _____?
Could I (possibly) _____?
Can I please _____?
Could I please _____?
May I (please) _____?
Would it be possible for me to _____?
Is it all right/okay (with you) if I _____?

I'd like to _____, if that's all right/okay
　　(with you).
Would it be all right/okay (with you) if
　　I _____ed?　　　　　　　　　9

Would you mind if I _____ed?
Would you object if I _____ed?
Would it bother you if I _____ed?
Do you mind if _____?　　　　　9

Granting . . .

Certainly.
Sure.
Of course.
By all means.
It's all right with me.
It's fine with me.
It's okay with me.　　　　　　　9

I wouldn't mind.
I don't mind.　　　　　　　　　9

Go (right) ahead.
Be my guest.　　　　　　　　　9

I guess so.
I suppose so.
I don't see (any reason) why not.　9

If you want to _____, it's
{
fine
all right
okay
} with me.　　　　　　　　　9

Denying . . .

I'd rather (that) you didn't.
I'd rather that you not.
I'd prefer it if you didn't.
I'd prefer that you not.
I'd prefer you not to.　　　　　9

_____ing isn't allowed/permitted.
You mustn't _____ (under any
　　circumstances).
We don't permit anyone to _____.
You're not supposed to _____.
You may not _____ (without
　　permission).　　　　　　　9

That's out of the question.　　9

I can't do that without _____'s
{
authorization.
permission.
approval.
consent.
agreement.
}　　　　　　　　　　　　9

Inquiring about Permissibility

Is _____ing allowed/permitted?
Is it okay to _____?
Is it all right to _____?
Are you allowed/permitted to _____?
Are people allowed to _____?
Do they allow/permit _____ing?
Do they allow people to _____?　9

Indicating Permissibility

I don't think _____ing is allowed/
　　permitted.
I don't think you're allowed/permitted
　　to _____.
I don't think people are allowed/
　　permitted to _____.

I don't think they allow/permit people
　　to _____.
I don't think they allow/permit you
　　to _____.　　　　　　　　　9

Yes. _____ _____.
[less certain]
I think so.
I believe so.
Yes, as far as I know.　　　　　9

No, _____ _____.
[less certain]
I don't think so.
I don't believe so.
Not as far as I know.　　　　　9

Persuading–Insisting

I mean it!
I'm (really) serious.
I'm being honest with you.　　　5

Listen!
Look!
(No,) really!
(No,) I mean it!
(No,) honestly!
(Oh,) come on!　　　　　　　8,9

I insist.　　　　　　　　　　　8

Let me, for a change.
Let me, for once.　　　　　　　8

There's no sense in your _____ing.
There's no reason (for you) to _____.
You don't have to _____.
You shouldn't have to _____.　8

Possibility/Impossibility

Expressing Possibility

I might _____.
I may _____.
I thought I might _____.
I thought I'd _____.　　　　　7

Preference

Inquiring about . . .

Would you
{
prefer _____?
rather have _____?
like _____?
}　　　　　　　　　　　　　6

Would you like to
Would you prefer to
Would you rather
Do you want to
Would you care to
}
_____
(or _____)?　　　　　6

How would you like it?　　　　6

Do you have any strong feelings
　　about it?
Do you have any feelings about it one
　　way or another?
Do you care one way or the other?
Do you have a preference?　　6

Expressing . . .

I'd prefer _____.
I'd rather have _____.
I'd like _____.　　　　　　　6

I'd prefer to _____.
I'd rather _____.
I'd like to _____.
I'd much rather _____.   6

I'd prefer not to _____.   6

I feel strongly about _____ing.   6

If you'd rather I didn't _____
    I won't.   6

Probability/Improbability

Expressing Probability

I'll probably _____.
I'll most likely _____.   7

Promising

Asking for a Promise

Can I { rely on / depend on / count on } you to _____?   7

Can I { depend on / count on / rely on / be sure of } that?   7

Promise?   7

Offering a Promise

Promise.
I promise I'll _____.
I promise to _____.   7

I promise (you) _____.
I assure you _____.
I guarantee (that) _____.
I give you my word _____.
You can be sure _____.   7

Absolutely.
Definitely.
Positively.   7

You can { rely on / depend on / count on } me.   7

I won't let you down.
I won't disappoint you.   7

Remembering/Forgetting

Inquiring about . . .

Don't you remember?
You remember.   3

Did you remember to _____?   3

Did you happen to remember to _____?
You didn't remember to _____,
    did you?
You didn't by any chance remember to
    _____, did you?   3

Indicating . . .

Oh, that one.   3

I forgot (all about it).
I completely forgot.
It (completely) slipped my mind.   3

Requests

Direct, Polite

Could I ask you a favor?
Could I ask you to _____?   9

Direct, More Polite

Could you possibly _____?
Could you (please) _____?
Could I (possibly) ask you to _____?
Would you be willing to _____?   2

Would you mind
Would it bother you   } if I _____ed?
Would it disturb you   6

Satisfaction/Dissatisfaction

Inquiring about . . .

How do you like _____?
What do you think of _____?   5

How did you like _____?   5

Did you (really) like it?   5

Are you { happy / satisfied / pleased } with it?   5

Is it _____ enough?   5

What seems to be the problem (with it)?
What seems to be the matter (with it)?
What's the problem (with it)?
What's the matter (with it)?
What's wrong (with it)?   5

Expressing Satisfaction

It's { fine. / very nice. / perfect. }   5

It's just what I { had in mind. / wanted. / was looking for. }   5

I wouldn't want it any _____er.   5

Expressing Dissatisfaction

It's too _____.   5

I really { expected it to be / thought it would be / hoped it would be } _____er.   5   5

It wasn't as _____ as I thought it
    would be.   5

Surprise–Disbelief

Assistant manager?!
They're going to make the park across
    the street into a parking lot?!   2,3

School isn't really going to be closed
    tomorrow, is it?   3

Oh?   9

You're kidding!
No kidding!
You're joking!
I don't believe it.
I can't believe it!
Oh, come on!
No!
That can't be!
You've got to be kidding!   3

Gee!
Boy!
Wow!   7

(Well,) how about that!
(Well,) what do you know!
(Well,) how do you like that!
(Well,) isn't that something!   9

Sympathizing

That's too bad!
That's a shame!
That's a pity!
What a shame!
What a pity!   2,7

I'm (very) sorry to hear about that.
I'm (very) sorry.
I'm so sorry.   2

Want–Desire

Inquiring about . . .

When do you want to _____?
Who would you like to _____?
What would you like to do?
How would you like me to _____?
Which _____ would you rather _____?
Where do you want _____ to
    _____?   6

Expressing . . .

I'd like _____.
I'll have _____.
I want _____.   6

I (really) don't feel like _____ing.
I'm not (really) in the mood to _____.
I don't think I'm in the mood
    to _____.   6

I'd (really) prefer not to _____.   6

_____ wants me to _____.   6

Scripts for Listening Exercises

Page 4

Listen and choose the best response.

1. Nice to meet you. What do you do?
2. I'm a doctor. What about you?
3. Which apartment do you live in?
4. How long have you been in the United States?
5. What's your major?
6. What kind of music do you like?

Page 5

Listen and choose the best conclusion.

1. A. Hi, John. I haven't seen you in a long time.
   B. I know. How have you been, Paul?
2. A. Hello. I don't think we've met. I'm Dr. Jones.
   B. How do you do? I'm Sam Smith. Nice to meet you.
3. A. I'm Tom. Nice to meet you.
   B. I'm pleased to meet you, too. My name is Sally.
4. A. My name's Kim. I'm from Korea. How about you?
   B. I'm Luis. I'm from Spain.
5. A. Ruth, whose office are you going to?
   B. Martha's.

Page 18

Listen and choose the answer that is closest in meaning to the sentence you have heard.

1. I have some good news!
2. You must be thrilled!
3. Oh, I'm happy to hear that.
4. You must be ecstatic!
5. I'm sorry to hear that.
6. You must be very upset.

Page 18

Listen and choose the best response.

1. I have some bad news.
2. I was just given a raise.
3. My parents are getting a divorce.
4. I was just offered a job at Harvard University.
5. I'm going to have to close my business.
6. I was rejected by the business school I applied to.
7. I was awarded the prize for best violinist in the orchestra.
8. I had to pay a thousand dollars to have my car repaired.

Page 35

Listen and decide where each conversation is taking place.

1. A. Hello. I'm looking for a warm sweater.
   B. How about this green one made in Scotland?

2. A. Which sport jacket should I wear to the interview?
   B. How about the one Uncle George gave you for your birthday?
3. A. Should I get the black tie or the blue one?
   B. Why don't you get the blue one?
4. A. Could I see the pocket-size camera in the leather case?
   B. Sure. Here it is. It's very inexpensive.
5. A. Which flag is the Japanese flag?
   B. It's the white one with the red sun in the middle.
6. A. Why don't you order the pie that Aunt Helen usually orders?
   B. You mean the one with apples and raisins in it?

Page 37

Listen and choose the answer that is closest in meaning to the sentence you have heard.

1. Can you tell me what it's like in Kyoto?
2. It's one of the most exciting places I know.
3. Can you tell me anything else?
4. What else would you like to know?
5. How are the people and the beaches?
6. As far as I'm concerned, you'll have a fantastic time there.
7. In my opinion, China is a beautiful place.
8. As a matter of fact, you're right.
9. If you ask me, the people there are very friendly.

Page 44

Listen and decide according to the intonation whether or not the speaker is surprised.

1. They're going to build a school across the street?!
2. She's just been promoted.
3. I'm going to get a raise?!
4. The mayor is coming to my office today.
5. You're going out of business?!
6. There's a rumor going around about me?!
7. I overheard a funny story.
8. You're fired.
9. I'm fired?!

Page 55

Listen and choose the best answer.

1. A. Excuse me, but would you mind turning down your radio? I'm trying to study.
   B. I'm sorry. I didn't hear you. What did you say?
2. A. Put your bags down. I'll carry them.
   B. I'm sorry. What did you say?

3. A. Please open your books to page thirty-two.
   B. I'm sorry. I didn't hear that. Would you mind repeating that?
4. A. Hand me a wrench, please. I want to put on this tire.
   B. Sure. Here it is.
5. A. Please turn down your stereo. I'm trying to sleep!
   B. I'm sorry. What did you say?
6. A. Turn right at the fourth light. Then take your third left.
   B. I'm sorry. I didn't quite catch that.
7. A. Please get me a copy of this report.
   B. I'm sorry. What did you say? I didn't hear you.

Page 60

Listen and follow the directions to different places on the map. Choose the letter that shows the place you're going to. The directions will always begin from *point X*.

1. A. Can you tell me how to get to the bank?
   B. Sure. Walk two blocks down Main Street and turn left. The bank is on the left.
2. A. Do you by any chance know where the train station is?
   B. Yes. Walk down Main Street three blocks, take a left, walk one block, and the train station is on the next block on the right.
   A. Thanks very much.
3. A. Could you possibly tell me where the bus stop is?
   B. I think so. Take your first left, walk to the corner, and the bus stop will be on your right.
4. A. Would you be able to tell me where Star Market is?
   B. Sure. Walk to the corner of Main and Central Street, take a left, and follow Central for two blocks. Turn left and the market is the building on the right.
5. A. Let me see if I understand. I go to Beach, turn left, and take a right on Ivy. The drug store is at the end of the block on the left. Right?
   B. That's right.
6. A. Do you know where the police station is?
   B. Uh-húh. Walk down Main Street to Beach. Follow Beach one block. Cross Ivy Street, and the police station is on the left.
   A. Thanks.

Page 65

Listen and choose the best response.

1. Could you possibly tell me where Grove Street is?
2. Walk two blocks and turn right. Have you got it?
3. Let me see. I turn right and then left?
4. First, pick up the receiver and put in the money.
5. Would you possibly be able to direct me to the nearest post office?
6. Then you mix these ingredients together. Are you with me so far?
7. Add oil, vinegar, spices, and a little water. Did you get all of that?
8. Form the bread into a long loaf. Okay so far?

Page 65

Listen and decide what process is being described.

1. First put in thirty-five cents. Then make your selection, and the candy will drop out of the machine.
2. First press eject. Then put in the tape. Then press play.
3. First write the date, then the name of the store and the amount of the purchase. Finally, sign your name.
4. First unlock the door. Then turn off the alarm. Then start the ignition.
5. First look through the lens. Then focus, and finally, push the button.
6. First unscrew the old bulb. Then get a new one and screw it into the lamp.

Page 70

Listen and decide where each conversation is taking place.

1. A. That was some performance!
   B. Thanks.
2. A. That was an excellent steak!
   B. Yes. I thought it was superb!
3. A. Your lecture was wonderful!
   B. Thanks for saying so.
4. A. Your presentation was absolutely fabulous!
   B. Thank you. It's nice of you to say that.
5. A. That was some game!
   B. Thank you.
6. A. Those photographs in your front hall are magnificent!
   B. Thank you for saying so.
7. A. That was some concert! You were terrific!
   B. It's nice of you to say that.
8. A. That was a pretty good report you gave on North American farms.
   B. Thank you.
9. A. That was a great picture you drew!
   B. Thanks. It's nice of you to say that.

Page 71

Listen and decide what the relationship between the two speakers is.

1. A. Emily is a wonderful student!
   B. Oh, I'm so glad to hear that.
2. A. I'm happy to tell you you're in excellent health!
   B. That's great! Thanks.
3. A. You did very well on your test!
   B. That's terrific! I was worried.
4. A. Am I really going to get that raise?
   B. Yes. Absolutely.
5. A. I'm going to have to give you a ticket.
   B. Oh, no!
6. A. The service was superb!
   B. Thank you, sir.
7. A. Are you sure you're innocent?
   B. Absolutely.
8. A. You did a fabulous job cleaning your room!
   B. Thanks.
9. A. I have a magnificent house to show you.
   B. Oh, that's great!

Page 73

Listen and decide what each customer is buying.

1. I'd like one that's not too firm, but not too soft either.
2. Do you have one that's not so heavy?
3. This isn't long enough.
4. These are too bulky.
5. Is this too tight?
6. I wouldn't want it any shorter.

Page 77

Listen and choose the answer that is closest in meaning to the sentence you have heard.

1. The movie wasn't as good as I thought it would be.
2. To tell you the truth, I was disappointed with my grades.
3. I really hoped the class wouldn't be so long.
4. To be honest with you, Howard was nicer than I thought he would be.
5. How come you were disappointed?
6. Well, honestly, the company was a little disappointed with Brian's work.
7. Linda's presentation was more interesting than I thought it would be.
8. John's tennis partner was more challenging than he had expected him to be.
9. To be honest with you, I thought it was terrible.
10. The baseball player wasn't very pleased with the score of the game.
11. The waterfalls weren't as exciting as I had expected.

Page 82

Listen and decide how Speaker B feels about Speaker A's suggestion.

1. A. How about American food tonight?
   B. Oh, I'm tired of American food.
2. A. Let's go skating today.
   B. Sure. That sounds good.
3. A. We could go sailing later.
   B. Oh, I'm afraid I don't enjoy sailing.
4. A. I guess you must be tired of going bicycling.
   B. No. On the contrary, I'd love to go bicycling.
5. A. Would you be interested in going dancing tonight?
   B. Well, I'm not really crazy about dancing.
6. A. One of my favorite places to go for ice cream is Charlie's.
   B. To tell the truth, I'm really sick of ice cream.
7. A. Let's go to a fancy restaurant tonight.
   B. Great!
8. A. If you don't like Indian food, we can go somewhere else.
   B. No. I love Indian food.
9. A. Then it's settled. We'll leave at eight o'clock.
   B. Well, how about nine thirty?

Page 95

Listen and decide where each conversation is taking place.

1. A. Where do you want to go to dinner after class?
   B. Oh, I don't care.
2. A. Here's the waiter. What kind of pizza should we order?
   B. Oh, it doesn't matter to me.
3. A. Would you like me to wrap up this plant for you, or do you want to take it the way it is?
   B. I don't know. It's all the same to me.
4. A. Where do you want me to put the desk?
   B. It doesn't make any difference. I guess right here is okay.
5. A. Which dessert on the menu do you like the best?
   B. I really don't have any preference.
6. A. It's getting late, and I'm tired. When do you want to leave this party?
   B. Oh, I don't care.
7. A. Where do you want me to put these reports?
   B. It doesn't make any difference. Over there is fine.
8. A. What color should we paint this basement?
   B. I don't really have any preference.

9. A. Let's order. How do you like your steak?
   B. I don't care. It's all the same to me.

Page 109

Listen and decide what the relationship between the two speakers is.

1. A. I promise I'll return the car by five o'clock.
   B. Okay. You don't have to hurry home.

2. A. You can count on me to do a good job.
   B. Good. We can use dependable people here at Westwood Medical Supply Company.

3. A. Can I count on you to write to me often, dear?
   B. Sure. I won't let you down.

4. A. Will we take off on time?
   B. Absolutely. Our flight will be right on time.

5. A. I'm relying on you to bring back my laptop computer before my next paper is due.
   B. Don't worry. I guarantee it'll be back by tomorrow night.

6. A. Now remember. I'm depending on you to close the book shop by six o'clock tonight.
   B. Don't worry. I'll take care of everything.

Page 117

Listen and choose the best response.

1. Hi! It's me.
2. Tell me, what are you doing this afternoon?
3. Where are you going next weekend?
4. If it's okay with you, I'll pick you up at seven o'clock.
5. I'm planning to go skiing today. Would you be interested in joining me?
6. I'm going to the museum this afternoon.

Page 119

Listen to the conversation and decide whether Speaker B's plan of action is *definite*, *probable*, or *possible*.

1. A. What are you going to do tonight?
   B. I'm not sure. I might go to a movie.

2. A. Have you decided where to go for your vacation?
   B. I'll probably go to Bermuda.

3. A. What are you going to order?
   B. Well, I thought I might try the scrambled eggs. I'm not sure yet.

4. A. Are you going to study English or German next semester?
   B. I may study English. I'm having a hard time deciding.

5. A. Are you going to ask for a raise?
   B. Absolutely!

6. A. I hear you're going to start your own business!
   B. Well, I've given it a lot of thought, and I've decided it's time to do it!

7. A. Which science course are you going to take?
   B. I'll most likely take Biology.

8. A. When are you going to retire?
   B. Well, I thought I'd stay one more year. I'm still thinking about it.

9. A. How are you going to pay for this suit?
   B. I'm going to charge it.

Page 119

Listen and choose the answer that is closest in meaning to the sentence you have heard.

1. I thought I might make an apple pie for dessert.
2. I'm thinking about taking Chinese.
3. I thought I'd make my father a sweater for his birthday.
4. I may go home early today.
5. I've been thinking about asking Ruth to the prom.
6. I might change my career soon.

Page 130

Listen and choose the best conclusion.

1. A. Mrs. Crawford, I'll turn off all the lights if you'd like.
   B. Okay. I'd appreciate that, Sally.

2. A. I don't mind driving to work today, Bob.
   B. No, that's all right, Mike. I like driving.

3. A. Judy, let me feed the baby for a change. You're always the one who feeds the baby.
   B. Okay. Thanks. That would be nice, Richard.

4. A. John, wouldn't you like me to go grocery shopping?
   B. No. Don't worry about it, Linda. I don't mind going shopping.

5. A. I'd be glad to write that memo if you'd like, Mr. Jones.
   B. No, that's okay. I don't mind writing it, Jack.

Page 131

Listen and choose the best response.

1. Lisa, do you need any help carrying those groceries?
2. Charlie, I see you're changing your tires. Need any help?
3. Would you mind helping me sweep out the garage?
4. Here, let me dry some of those dishes.
5. I see you're cleaning out the attic. Do you want any help?
6. Larry, can I give you a hand with those skis?
7. My house hasn't been painted in a long time, so I thought I'd paint it this weekend.

8. Oh, no! My car is stuck in the snow!
9. Mr. Thompson, I'd be happy to finish up those technical drawings for you.
10. Are you sure you don't mind helping me?

Page 134

Listen and choose the answer that is closest in meaning to the sentence you have heard.

1. Would you like me to carry those books for you, Fred?
2. Oh, thanks for offering, but I don't need any help.
3. Look! I insist! You're not cleaning the basement by yourself!
4. I'd be glad to help you adjust the position of that picture.
5. Well, okay. You can help, but I really don't want to put you to any trouble.
6. Oh, it's no trouble at all. I'm happy to lend you a hand.
7. There's no sense in your chopping all those carrots by yourself!

Page 137

Listen carefully for specific details and answer the question at the end of each conversation.

1. A. Hello. May I help you?
   B. Yes. I'm looking for a food processor for my father. He loves to cook, and it's his birthday tomorrow.
   A. I'm afraid we're out of food processors.
   B. Oh, that's too bad!
   A. But we expect some in by next week.
   B. Hmm. I'm afraid that's too late. I need it by tomorrow. Thanks anyway.

What was the customer looking for?

2. A. Can I assist you?
   B. Yes. I'm looking for a pair of brown leather shoes like these in size thirteen.
   A. Well, we have them in size thirteen, but we only have them in black. Would you like me to get them for you?
   B. Sure, I'd appreciate that.

What is the salesperson going to show the customer?

3. A. Patty, do you want me to walk the dog?
   B. No. Don't worry about it, Frank. I don't mind walking the dog. I like the exercise.
   A. Listen! You're always the one who walks the dog. Let me, for a change.
   B. Well, okay. Thanks. It's nice of you to offer.

Why does Frank want to walk the dog?

4. A. Hello. Can I help you?
   B. Yes. I'm looking for a Flexible Flyer sled.
   A. Oh, I'm afraid we don't have any Flexible Flyers in stock anymore. I believe they've stopped making them.
   B. Oh. What a pity!
   A. Well, is there anything else I can help you with?
   B. I guess not, but thanks anyway.

Why didn't the store have Flexible Flyers?

5. A. Hi. May I help you?
   B. Yes. I'm looking for a pet for my child.
   A. How old is he?
   B. He's six and a half.
   A. Well, we have fish, hamsters, dogs, and cats.
   B. Do you have any birds?
   A. No, I'm afraid we're out of birds, but we expect to get some in next week.
   B. Okay, I'll come back then.

What animals did the pet store have in stock?

6. A. Hi, Vicky. I see you're planting your garden.
   B. Yes. It's time to put in the seeds.
   A. Well, can I give you a hand?
   B. Sure. If it's no trouble.
   A. No, not at all. I'd be happy to help. And anyway, I love being outside.
   B. Thanks. I appreciate that.

Where did this conversation take place?

Page 148

Listen and choose the best response.

1. Is taking pictures allowed here?
2. Are you allowed to pet the animals at the zoo?
3. Is using a dictionary permitted during the TOEFL test?
4. Are people allowed to walk on the grass here at the Public Garden?
5. Excuse me, sir. Do they permit hunting here in the mountains?
6. Is it okay to sleep on the beach overnight?
7. Pardon me. Are you allowed to climb on those rocks?

8. Do they permit stores to be open on Sundays in this state?
9. Are you allowed to touch the sculptures at this exhibit?
10. Excuse me. Are people permitted to have picnics here?
11. Is eating allowed in the library?
12. Is it okay to park in this handicapped area?

Page 156

Listen and decide what the relationship between the two speakers is.

1. A. Would you mind if I turned up the stereo?
   B. No, I wouldn't mind.

2. A. Would it bother you if I took a picture of the performance?
   B. No, not at all.

3. A. Is it all right with you if I make fish for dinner?
   B. By all means. That sounds great!

4. A. Do you mind if I try a new dive?
   B. No, of course not. Go right ahead!

5. A. I'd like to do a few tests on your husband, if that's all right with you.
   B. It's all right with me. I don't think he'll object.

6. A. Would you object to our visiting a few of my former students on our honeymoon?
   B. No, I don't mind.

7. A. If you'd rather I didn't have a pet in the apartment, I won't.
   B. No, that's okay. It's fine with me.

8. A. Is it okay to use my dictionary on the test?
   B. Certainly. Be my guest!

Page 159

Listen and decide whether the second speaker's response is positive or negative.

1. A. Would you mind if I turned on the radio?
   B. Well, I'd rather you didn't. I'm trying to sleep.

2. A. Is chewing gum allowed at camp?
   B. I think so.

3. A. Can I enter the laboratory without permission?
   B. I don't think so.

4. A. Would you object if I started eating before you? I'm starving!
   B. No. Go right ahead!

5. A. Do you mind if I take Johnny to the zoo after twelve o'clock?
   B. No, of course not!

6. A. Do they allow men on that floor of the dormitory?
   B. I don't believe so.

7. A. Could I please have an ice cream sundae?
   B. Certainly.

8. A. Would it be possible for me to skip class on Friday?
   B. No. We're having a quiz on Friday.

9. A. Is it all right if I use the telephone for a while?
   B. I suppose so.

10. A. Mark, may I borrow your new CD?
    B. I guess so. Why not?

11. A. Would you mind if I moved that picture and put it somewhere else?
    B. No, not at all.

12. A. Would it be all right if I put away the puzzle you've been working on?
    B. Actually, I'd prefer it if you wouldn't.

Index

Functions and Conversation Strategies

Advice–Suggestions, 78, 80–81
Agreement, 122–123
Apologizing, 7, 158, 160
Appreciation, 128, 129, 132–133, 140, 142
Asking for and Reporting Additional Information, 25, 36, 46–47
Asking for and Reporting Information, 2–3, 7, 10–11, 16, 17, 20–21, 25, 28–29, 36, 38, 42, 43, 46–47, 58–59, 62–63
Asking for Repetition, 54, 56, 58–59, 62–63
Attracting Attention, 138, 150

Certainty/Uncertainty, 38, 42, 43, 116
Checking and Indicating Understanding, 58–59, 62–63
Complaining, 74, 76, 78
Complimenting, 68, 69
Congratulating, 16, 20–21

Deduction, 16
Denying/Admitting, 158
Describing, 24, 25, 34, 36
Directions–Location, 58–59, 60
Disappointment, 76, 110–111

Focusing Attention, 36, 122–123

Gratitude, 68, 128, 129, 136, 138, 140, 142, 146–147, 150, 152
Greeting People, 2–3, 6

Hesitating, 28–29, 98–99, 152

Identifying, 10–11, 34
Indifference, 94, 96
Initiating a Topic, 10–11, 16, 17, 43, 114, 140
Initiating Conversations, 2–3, 7, 116, 122–123
Instructing, 56, 58–59, 62–63
Intention, 114, 116, 118, 120, 122–123
Introductions, 2–3, 6
Invitations, 116

Likes/Dislikes, 68, 69, 80–81

Offering to Do Something, 128
Offering to Help, 129, 132–133, 136, 138

Permission, 146–147, 150, 154–155, 158, 160, 162–163
Persuading–Insisting, 69, 128, 132–133, 140, 154–155
Possibility/Impossibility, 118
Preference, 86, 88, 90–91, 98–99
Probability/Improbability, 116
Promising, 106, 107, 110–111, 118

Remembering/Forgetting, 34, 40
Requests, 24, 54, 96, 152, 160

Satisfaction/Dissatisfaction, 72, 74, 76
Surprise/Disbelief, 16, 42, 43, 114, 150
Sympathizing, 17, 20–21, 110–111

Want–Desire, 86, 88, 90–91, 94, 98–99

Grammar Structures

Adjectives, 19, 24, 25, 34, 36, 68, 69, 72, 74, 75, 76
And/But, 26

Can, 138, 152
Comparatives, 72, 74, 76
Could, 152

Declarative Sentences with Question Intonation, 43
Demonstrative Adjectives, 132–133

Embedded Questions, 38, 39, 58–59, 118
Enough, 72, 73, 74

Future: Going to, 114
Future: Will, 106, 107, 108, 116

Gerunds, 54, 80–81, 88, 90–91, 114, 115, 116, 118, 122–123, 128, 132–133, 140, 142, 146–147, 148, 150, 160, 162–163

Imperatives, 58–59, 62–63, 150
Indirect Objects, 34, 140, 141
Infinitives, 80–81, 88, 114, 115, 116, 120, 122–123, 146–147, 148, 150, 160, 162–163

May, 152
Might, 118
Must, 16, 17, 19, 162–163

Negative Questions, 7, 80–81

One/Ones, 10–11, 13, 34, 35

Partitives, 62–63, 86, 87
Passives, 16, 17, 18, 40, 129, 138
Past Continuous Tense, 46–47
Past Continuous to Express Future Intention, 120
Past Tense, 46–47
Possessive Adjectives, 20–21
Present Continuous Tense to Express Habitual Action, 78
Present Perfect Tense, 88, 120
Pronouns, 20–21

Question Formation, 56

Relative Clauses with Who, 10–11, 128, 142
Relative Clauses with Whose, 10–11

Sequence of Tenses, 38, 40, 41, 54, 96, 110–111, 112, 154–155, 158
Short Answers, 146–147
Simple Present Tense, 28–29, 38
Singular/Plural, 80–81, 136
Superlatives, 36, 39

Tag Questions, 42, 44
Tense Review, 17, 20–21
Too/Enough, 72, 73, 74
Two–Word Verbs, 106, 108

Used to, 10–11

Want + Object + Infinitive, 90–91, 92, 128
Whether, 96
WH–ever words, 94, 95
WH–Questions, 2–3, 5, 56, 57
Would, 10–11, 54, 58–59, 74, 80–81, 86, 88, 96, 98–99, 116, 120, 128, 129, 132–133, 154–155